EMILY BRONTE

KEY
WOMEN
WRITERS
EDITOR: SUE ROE

EMILY BRONTE

STEVIE DAVIES

Lecturer in English Literature
University of Manchester

HARVESTER · WHEATSHEAF

NEW YORK   LONDON   TORONTO   SYDNEY   TOKYO

First published in Great Britain in 1988 by
Harvester · Wheatsheaf,
66 Wood Lane End,
Hemel Hemsptead, Hertfordshire, HP2 4RG

A division of
Simon & Schuster International Group

Printed and bound in Great Britain by
Billing and Sons Ltd.

British Library Cataloguing in Publication Data

Davies, Stevie, 1946–
Emily Brontë.—(Key women writers).
1. Fiction in English. Brontë, Emily,
1818–1848. Critical studies
I. Title   II. Series
823′.8
ISBN 0-7108-1024-5
ISBN 0-7108-1187-X Pbk

1 2 3 4 5   92 91 90 89 88

To Bill

The Book of Ruth 1:16-17

Titles in the Key Women Writers Series

Key Women Writers
Series Editor: Sue Roe

The *Key Women Writers* series has developed in a spirit of challenge, exploration and interrogation. Looking again at the work of women writers with established places in the mainstream of the literary tradition, the series asks, in what ways can such writers be regarded as feminist? Does their status as canonical writers ignore the notion that there are ways of writing and thinking which are specific to women? Or is it the case that such writers have integrated within their writing a feminist perspective which so subtly maintains its place that these are writers who have, hitherto, been largely misread?

In answering these questions, each volume in the series is attentive to aspects of composition such as style and voice, as well as to the ideas and issues to emerge out of women's writing practice. For while recent developments in literary and feminist theory have played a significant part in the creation of the series, feminist theory represents no specific methodology, but rather an opportunity to broaden our range of responses to the issues of history, psychology and gender which have always engaged women writers. A new and creative dynamics between a woman critic and her female subject has been made possible by recent developments in feminist theory, and the series seeks to reflect the important critical insights which have emerged out of this new, essentially feminist, style of engagement. It is not always the case that literary theory can be directly transposed from its sources in other disciplines to the practice of reading writing by women. The series investigates the possibility that a distinction may need to be made between feminist politics and the literary criticism of women's writing which has not, up to now, been sufficiently emphasized. Feminist reading, as well as feminist writing, still needs to be constantly interpreted and re-interpreted. The complexity and range of choices implicit in this procedure are represented throughout the series. As works of criticism, all the volumes in the series represent wide-ranging and creative styles of discourse, seeking at all times to express the particular resonances and perspectives of individual women writers.

Sue Roe

Contents

Acknowledgements

I should like to acknowledge here my debt to Irene Tayler, Professor of English Literature at the Massachusetts Institute of Technology, who has shared with me her incomparable Brontë scholarship and her brilliant intuitions into Charlotte's and Emily's novels and poetry. Even more, I offer her my thanks for the gift of her loving friendship.

The work I have done in collaboration with William B. Hunter, Emeritus Professor of English Literature at the University of Houston, on Milton's Muse, has by a natural process fed in to the present work on 'Milton's daughter'. I acknowledge, with wonder and gratitude, his boundless resources of intellectual energy and wisdom, upon which I have been permitted to draw without restraint.

I should like to record my gratitude to Alan Shelston, senior lecturer in English Literature at the University of Manchester, for the benefit I have received from his far-reaching and humane mind in conversations on nineteenth-century fiction going back over twenty years.

Finally, I owe my thanks to Rosalie Wilkins for sustaining my spirits during the writing of the book, and to Katherine Spearman for shared visits to Haworth and the moors, which I shall always think of as being linked with her.

S. Davies
7 June 1987

Introduction

The aggressive silence with which Emily Brontë guarded the originality of her gift—comparable with the reclusiveness espoused by Emily Dickinson to defend as extraordinary a power—is a ruthless final barrier to interpretative penetration of her world: refusal of mediation. Even her near kin, Charlotte, registers an ultimate sense of the unknown and unknowable as she seeks to translate her uncivil sister into the received dialect. As 'a native and nursling of the moors... her native hills were far more to her than a spectacle; they were what she lived in, and by, as much as the wild birds, their tenants, or as the heather, their produce'.[1] As one with the community of 'wild birds... heather', Emily is figured as an isolated foreigner from the human community, a permanently exilic figure absorbed in its commerce with its native wilderness. Charlotte invests Emily's image with the allure of the incommunicable. She seals her in to a status as 'native and nursling' as dependent (on nature) as it is independent of, and indifferent to, the urban community. It is this intransigent otherness which generations of readers have confronted with obsessive curiosity in *Wuthering Heights*, recognising there a language which brings with it an aura of intense familiarity (as if it spoke of something we had once known and since forgotten) and a hoarding inwardness, impervious to the literary interpreter's immemorial desire to break codes and betray secrets. Our representative in the novel, Lockwood, confronting that system of Chinese boxes which is the narrative architectonic,[2] is garrulous and voyeuristic *homo sapiens* who expounds and participates in a riddle the nuance of whose cryptic language he cannot read. *Wuthering Heights*, more than any work of English fiction, has impressed its readers with a sense of numinous forbidden territory. The Janus of authorial irony firmly refuses right of entry to the trespassing reader.

To forbid entry is, of course, a standing and enticing invitation to the outsider to try to get in. Lockwood's penetration of the Heights[3]—in at the front door, the kitchen, Catherine's bedroom, her bed, her books, the communal dream—also enables our access to the meanings the novel is prepared to divulge. Stranded with the inadequate narrator in a story which is perceived by fragments, surmises, dreamwork, guesswork, espionage and secondary or tertiary glimpses of events, we are taunted by an art which arouses desire as a craving appetite for knowledge which it scorns to allay. Resort to narrative authority is impractical in a work dedicated to thwarting the reader's desire for comfort.[4] Long before modernist writers like Katherine Mansfield, Dorothy Richardson and Virginia Woolf were to create 'a deliberate female aesthetic, which transformed the feminine code of self-sacrifice into an annihilation of the narrative self',[5] Emily Brontë had splintered narrative unity into a multiplicity of dispersals bound together by the deepest irony—not, I take it, as a killing into art of the code of repressions fathered upon her by society, but as raising an eternal fortification against that society. It has often been noted that the novel's major (and symbolic) location and concentration of meaning is the interior of a house:[6] I will add that this interiority, with its compression of psychic energy, at once menacing and compelling, resembles the intramural structuring of the mind itself, sealed in a state of private thought, of which a few traces stray out into the general continuum. Lockwood's double dream appears to transmit scraps of this perpetual silent soliloquy. In condemning the interpreter to a status of eternal outsider and trespasser, the novel's spherical, self-engrossed composition is a speaking assertion of the primacy of self, hallowing its own inwardness as unknown and unknowable ground. *Wuthering Heights* as a stronghold for self presents the reflection of a single mind in a state of artistic security, as impervious to anxiety of influence as it is to anxiety of interpretation.

The author labelled herself pseudonymously 'Ellis Bell': the chiming of these male-sounding syllables denied to the ear of her contemporaries the knowledge of her gender, as did the flaunting of chastely feminine decorums, whether artistic or moral, by her novel. The earliest reviews of *Wuthering Heights* do not concentrate on the sex of the author, whose originality baffled all conception of gender-distinction in its challenge to the boundaries of what is human and non-human. The novel had broken new ground for the species—the soul—the community of the English language. To make such a breakthrough implied, according to the culture prevailing amongst 'Ellis Bell's' readership, that one's gender must be male. *The Examiner* assumes the novel's

3

masculinity: 'We detest the affectation and effeminate frippery which is but too frequent in the modern novel', but regrets the search for the 'coarse and loathesome' which Ellis Bell's imagination undertakes.[7] These reviews were far more complimentary than Charlotte Brontë in her *Biographical Notice of Ellis and Acton Bell* was to maintain: their key word is *power*. Their terms of approval are 'power and originality'; their distrust sounds in epithets like 'rude . . . unfinished . . . careless'.[8] The American opinion that 'the writer was not accustomed to the society of gentlemen' but is 'unmannered from want of delicacy of perception, or cultivation, or ill-mannered intentionally'[9] never thinks to speculate as to whether the rude author had kept company with ladies. Critics' preoccupation with responding to the seismic qualities of the novel prevented the squandering of energy on the current fad of gender-speculation. By the 1870s and 1880s, when Emily Brontë was being reassessed as a greater genius than Charlotte, remarks about her sex still failed to undermine and distort critical valuation in the damaging way they affected Charlotte's work. Reference to Emily's gender seems either bemused or exclamatory. 'From what unfathomed recesses of her intellect did this shy, nervous, untrained girl produce such characters as those which hold the foremost place in her story?' asked Reid in 1877. 'Strange and appalling thesis to be expounded by an English girl!' exclaimed Peter Bayne in 1881;[10] but he went on to compare her work with Homer's *Iliad* and Shakespeare's *Lear*. Emily Brontë strikingly and uniquely offered the nineteenth century no obvious means for using her gender as a way of dominating (and hence depreciating) the novel. Readers found there no feminist protest, no engagement with the woman question, and indeed no expression of authorial opinion on any topic.

Introduction

Victorian reaction registers the success of Emily Brontë's resistance to the twin tyrannies of influence and exegesis. Tradition is the obvious way of gaining access to an unfamiliar literary text: we seek to recognise the verbal patterns reinscribed (with significant differences) by the individual author, inherited from our fathers. But Emily Brontë's appropriation of her sources displays (*nearly* invariably) curiously centripetal quality: a certain nullity of linguistic inflection neutralises the allusiveness of extrinsic material, so that it fails to refer us back to its origins within an explanatory tradition. This guilt-lessness of debt in *Wuthering Heights* is one of the factors—along with the diffusions and dispersals of its narrative strategy—so uncomfortable to readers seeking access to its autonomy. If such autonomy had been less immaculate, we may be sure that the experienced élite of Victorian reviewers would have broken the shell of disinterest which holds *Wuthering Heights* intact. In a comparable way, *Wuthering Heights* can be discerned to have begotten no literary tradition, whether male or female. It is an original: yet it cannot breed.

The rage for detailed inside information about the personal life of the sisters, mounting in the nineteenth century and continuing in this, exacerbated the desire for penetration but in no way facilitated access. Post-Freudian criticism, psychoanalysing the author through the novel, has its roots in the diagnoses and 'incestuous' readings of *Wuthering Heights* fashionable in the earlier part of this century.[11] The most perceptive and illuminating accounts of the work—by Sanger, Cecil, Dorothy Van Ghent[12]—were not specifically feminist; and, indeed, its secretive modernity could still in 1966 baffle the full-scale feminist enquiry made by Inge-Stina Ewbank in *Their Proper Sphere*, eliciting the opinion that Emily Brontë's world is intrinsically ungendered, because it is the world of a poet.[13] In the 1970s and 1980s such a view began to seem archaic. Post-deconstructionist feminism has insisted on the author's gender as *the* determining factor in the conception and meaning of the work. Gilbert and Gubar's brilliantly innovative *The Madwoman in the Attic* (1979) galvanised a generation of critics with its account of the 'anxiety of influence' (after Harold Bloom)[14] under which Emily Brontë as 'Milton's daughter' laboured to produce her revisionary counter-myth. The structures within language itself and literary tradition are understood in this wave of feminism as male artifacts, designed to perpetuate a patriarchal society, within which foreign inheritance the female author must forge her own identity. Latterly, a Marxist line of criticism has joined with a deconstructive, psychoanalytic and 'feminist' influence: in James Kavanagh's *Emily Brontë* we are arrested by the bizarre phenomenon of a 'feminism' dominated by the bearded patriarchs of literary criticism, Freud and Marx, and claiming to reveal her as 'raped away in the world of her own creating' by the father's pen/penis.[15] Such phallocentric 'feminism' represents the degeneration of a critical tradition, in which the quest for insight has become a desecrating voyeurism.

The figure of Milton stands at the centre of the current debate, Gilbert and Gubar's appraisal of Emily Brontë as 'Milton's daughter' bearing to the present generation the status of a credo. To question it would involve resisting the authority of Bloom's *Anxiety of Influence* which stands behind it, and behind him the more massive authority of Freud and the Oedipus complex. Hence Gilbert and Gubar exemplify the ambiguous response to male traditions and institutionalised beliefs to which they are indebted, which they describe as presenting a dispossessing inheritance to the writing daughters. Few literary critics are scientifically trained, of course, so as to be competent to verify or challenge the Freudian reading of the psyche. Nevertheless, it is open to us (starting, perhaps, from the texture of the words on the page in *Wuthering Heights*) to imagine a model, or models, of the creative psyche less replete with anxiety and representing less an *agon* of oppression than is currently allowed. In the present work I emphasise the unusual degree of exemption, or immunity, in Emily Brontë from what the twentieth century has decided are the 'necessary' conditions of human nature. The artist is always in some sense a deviation from the norm. Emily's singularity may be imagined as that of a *lusus naturae* whose strategies of self-concealment may have resisted or circumvented the stress with which 'Milton's daughter' is supposed to have agonised her way into print. Doubtless, this may turn out to be a matter of emphasis. But it is not inconceivable that Milton may appear more of an imaginative bogey to Gilbert and Gubar than he ever did to Emily Brontë. We can hypothesise an enabling Milton, whose punitive 'fatherhood' was a good excuse for the excitement of rebellion and whose own revolutionary Puritanism furnished the vindication for such heretical dissidence. Such a Milton could be seized on as a liberator to his unimplicated female descendant, especially as his immediate influence had already been mitigated by the resistance of the Romantics, and especially Byron, the implications of whose theology I shall examine. Milton, of course, was a republican and regicide: Emily Brontë was a Royalist. She is the 'little King' of the early games—the legitimate inheritor and possessor of her own creative kingdom. In one childhood game Emily is recorded as impersonating the monarch to be restored, Charles II, hiding in the royal oak at Worcester from the Cromwellian army, the imagined tree being impersonated by that which grew beneath the window at her father's house. 'All the princes and princesses of the Royalty are at the Palace of Instruction', runs her diary paper of 1841,[16] the Gondal game possibly recalling the detention of Charles II and the rest of the king's children: the exiled pretender who is really the legitimate monarch would be a richly fortifying myth for a girl-child convinced of her own innate royalty and knowing that she must eventually be restored to her own kingdom. The republicans in Gondal seem to have continued consistently victorious; the Royalists a remnant, subject to 'Instruction', the brain-washing education of the powers that be. But as 'Chief Genius' and 'little King', their creator perceives her royalty and legitimacy as a state extraneous to the game's captivities. Emily Brontë plays more than king as the artist of her literary world: she plays God, in her strict truancy from the object of her making.

I am imagining here not the mythic Titan of whom Mrs Gaskell told in her *Life of Charlotte Brontë*,[17] nor the Emily figured in Charlotte's *Shirley*, whose shrill or pompous protestations ('I would wish to remind him . . .', 'No, by the pure Mother of God . . .' [see pp. 31–2 below]) confess Milton's fatal incursion into Shirley's heart of hearts. What I am guessing at is an insularity combined with an imaginative comprehensiveness and aberrant structuring of perceptions (perhaps innate) which could identify with the liberating spirit in Milton, with cavalier disregard for the sexual or political infringement he sought of her right to appropriate the freedoms he claimed for men. Sealed in her art-world, the moor strategically placed for escape above the house, no domesticating and limiting mother to weaken her capacity for identification with whatever sex she chose to impersonate at a particular moment, polite society at a

safe distance, and a father who seems to have selected
her as an honorary boy to be trusted with fire-arms in
defence of the weak, Emily Brontë's life exemplifies a
rough joy in itself, its war-games, its word-games and its
power to extend its own structuring vision out upon the
given world. Joy in language—a child's vigorous and
unchidden affirmations through the native tongue—
stems from right of conquest and bequest. Confidence in
her virtuoso mode of address signals (early readers were
astonished at Emily Brontë's early maturity—as if *Lear*
rather than *Love's Labour's Lost* had been Shakespeare's
first play)[18] not solely years of private practice in her art
but also her unreserved assertion of her right to speak,
in plain English. No Victorian author is more plain and
downright in his seizure of possession of root Anglo-
Saxon; her mother-tongue.

It is doubtful whether Emily Brontë could be imagined
as accepting without mockery the proposition which has
become axiomatic in our own day that language is a
universally masculine artifact.[19] Such a position
affronts women by ascribing to them a witless pusillan-
imity within society. Women have always made language.
They have handed it on from generation to generation,
on behalf of the race. Emily Brontë's novelistic technique
echoes an oral tradition of literature passed from mouth
to (mainly female) mouth: the main tellers of the story of
Wuthering Heights are Nelly, Catherine I, Isabella, Zillah.
A sophisticated narrative structure derives its force and
immediacy from roots in the private gossip of small,
compact and insular communities whose refusal of the
outside world is also denial of the dominance of
competitive linguistic, social and tribal custom. 'Mim!
mim! mim!' says Joseph in imitation of Isabella's received
pronunciation, 'Minching un' munching! Hah can Aw
tell whet ye say?',[20] Emily Brontë may well have inclined

9

to the view that appropriation is nine-tenths of the law: you take the language you want and make it your own, twisting it to your own needs and purposes. The world of *Wuthering Heights* is near to anarchy, each one speaking his or her own language: law-breaking is normalised into standard practice. The principle of riot is never far from the surface, exemplified perhaps in Lockwood's dream of the saturnalia in the chapel which 'resounded with rappings and counter-rappings. Every man's hand was against his neighbour' (p. 22). Relish for anarchy is everywhere felt in the confident narrative style of *Wuthering Heights*, the spree of words, the sense of authorial power through the game of language: power to release a violent exodus of words, power to dam that overbearing energy. The 'little King' reigns over her material unimpaired, sole despot of the art-world that began as a child's game, secluded from the society which, as Emily Brontë grew in consciousness, she must have perceived as a threat to the foundations of her freedom of speech and the joy she had taken in it. Those who argue that language is essentially a paternal inheritance have, I think, never accounted for the phenomenon of the *Muttersprache*, which constitutes most children's initiation into language. For the first five years of life, the mother has traditionally authorised language: the pattern of communication (and communication-as-joy, the art-world) is set by her, within the theatre of a bonded reality. The first generation of children in *Wuthering Heights* may be seen protecting an exclusive right of play, together with a right of primitive utterance, symbolised by Catherine's and Heathcliff's repudiation of the books forced on them, and by Cathy's marginal diary in the Testament. We can, it is true, see this as a testament to the obliquity and marginal status of the female life: but turn it round, and it becomes an act of conquest—the

Father's words remain untranscribed and unread within the framing text of *Wuthering Heights*, his church falls down, his children go to the bad; the daughter's words, reclaimed from the shadow of 'some quarter of a century back' (p. 18), are brought to light, are read and achieve success: 'I began, forthwith, to decypher her faded hieroglyphics'.

The language of *Wuthering Heights* has a variety of well-attested sources in literary tradition: Shakespeare, Milton, the Bible, Scott, Byron. But one of its deepest roots is in the genres of English literature which are most verifiably related to the female experience: sung poetry such as lullaby, ballad, folk-tale and nursery story, and last but not least, gossip (originally *god sib*, good speech, spiritual kin). Nelly sings a snatch of a ballad as a lullaby to Hareton. She is mediating between the soil—Mother Earth, where his earthly mother is buried—and the baby, in the appropriate voice. In Emily Brontë's household, Tabby had served as a living linguistic medium of a speech that was original and native: it was a fostering voice, not kin but akin through identity of gender, eternal, powerful, protective and (to Emily) funny. In Emily's Diary Paper of 1834, we can see oral tradition in the act of transcription. Emily takes Tabby down onto paper verbatim: 'Come Anne pilloputate . . . Ya pitter pottering there instead of pilling a potate'.[21] We observe that Tabby's utterance takes the imperative voice, denotes accusation and aspires (in Emily's non-committal record) to the condition of nonsense. This glorious levity at the heart of the domestic world—the sanctum of the sisters, profoundly private despite the incursions of the paternal Voice ('papa opened the parlour door and gave Branwell a letter saying here Branwell read this and show it to your aunt and Charlotte')—implies the expansion of space for being oneself in one's native tongue—a prolongation of childhood liberties. In *Wuthering Heights* Hareton does not fall into uncouth language until he leaves Nelly's care and is initiated into the world of 'Daddy' and 'Devil daddy'.

If we need a psychological model to elucidate the eccentric integrity of Emily Brontë's work, it may act as a corrective to the excessively Oedipal times in which we live, in which *all* variation of perception is diagnosed in terms of Freudian sexual psychology, to allude to modern theories of perception based on the physiology of the brain. The specialisation of the right and left lobes of the brain in relation to specific intellectual functions, and in relation to individual-handedness,[22] makes an interesting point of speculation in relation to so deviant a consciousness. It is possible that Emily Brontë was left-handed (linking her perceptions naturally with the right-hand lobe of the brain, specialised for spatial, holistic, analogic, intuitive and non-temporal modes of knowing). Certainly her handwriting was late in forming, and, when formed, remained cramped and poor, possibly implying the difficulties faced by left-handers in pushing the pen across the page. Edward Chitham has also suggested Emily's left-handedness from the posture of a self-portrait on the 1845 diary-paper.[23] The calligraphic phenomenon is in itself unimportant, except insofar as it supplies a hint: what is significant is Emily Brontë's habit of *reversal*. In a dualistic world, her invariable practice is to reverse the norms. She seems to have adopted and uniquely maintained, against all the pressure of conditioning, a minority view of reality, diametrically opposed to that assumed by the accepted conventions of her culture. If we imagine her work as revealing a 'sinistral' rather than a 'dextral' structuring of perception, comparable with that which is found in extreme left-handers who in early childhood write naturally backwards ('mirror-writing'), we have a model for viewing the atypical spatial and conceptual character of *Wuthering Heights* as pertaining to an innate mode of perception unrelated to Oedipal anxiety. I posit this 'sinistral' way of viewing the structures of reality, and the mimesis of such apprehended structure in artistic composition, as the product of an idiosyncratic approach to experience which defended itself with extraordinary determination against the persuasions of consensus judgment which affect every growing child. This habit of mind, which manifested itself as a kind of holy cussedness or creative bolshevism, was sustained until—literally—her dying day: in response to his medical advice, Charlotte cautioned W.S. Williams only a month before Emily died:

> It is best usually to leave her to form her own judgment, and *especially* not to advocate the side you wish her to favour; if you do, she is sure to lean in the opposite direction, and ten to one will argue herself into non-compliance.
> (*Shakespeare Head Life and Letters* II, p. 286, 22 Nov. 1848)

Artistically, this abnormal resistance to influence in its debilitating form seems to have freed Emily to enjoy the power to make an arrogant and excited adoption of influence into herself, but frequently to reverse it, 'mirror-writing' what she received. The Christian myth activated in her an anti-Christian myth. Patriarchal norms implied a matriarchal alternative. It is interesting to reflect that one of Emily's favourite sentence-structures takes the rhetorical form of the chiasmus, the second half reversing the first (see pp. 98, 146 below). Indeed, the total structure of *Wuthering Heights* could be viewed as chiastic. Such a tendency to reverse 'reality' is found in all children: it is often called naughtiness, and discouraged. In art it may produce a saturnalian effect; in adult life a sense of the norms as risible. We shall see both these principles operating extensively within the narrative of *Wuthering Heights* (see pp. 47–8 below). Adopted as a way of life, of course, this way madness is said to lie, according to the consensus; and also what is called genius. Emily Brontë's great intellectual strengths were music, mathematics, art, logic—all skills requiring the intuitions of the right-hand lobe of the brain (linked with the left hand).[24] 'She should have been a man—a great navigator', said M. Heger of Emily, in the language of contemporary prejudice. 'Her powerful reason would have deduced new spheres of discovery from the knowledge of the old; and her strong, imperious will would never have been daunted by opposition or difficulty; never have given way but with life.' Heger, however, seasoned his account of Emily as nautical hero *manquée* with the disapproving remark that, by comparison with the unselfish Charlotte, the younger sister was egotistical and exacting.[25] The schoolmaster's praise is the unconscious corollary of his blame: the former indicates his pupil's innate dominance of structures, her spatial awareness, the latter draws attention to the asocial non-conformity of the temperament which was able to achieve such dominance.

A sinistral view of reality would shape its perceptions into reversals or radical modifications of the norm without necessarily being conscious of how peculiar this might appear to those who were satisfied with a version of orthodoxy. For instance, a radical non-conformity in relation to gender-roles might be incorporated into a work of art without the necessity of a pre-existent theoretical basis. When we extrapolate such theories from the text, our deductions are always translations from the art-language into the common tongue. Because

Introduction

Emily Brontë's work does not mediate or interpret itself to the reader, it presents itself as the object of knowledge rather than the vehicle of knowledge. There is a sublime innocence about Emily's inability (recorded by Charlotte) to understand what quality it was in her writing to which the critics took exception.[26] Her lifelong failure to normalise her view of reality made it inevitable that she should be seen, in art as in life, as a misfit and, since this society was male-dominated, her uniqueness—*faute de mieux*—realises itself as a bias against patriarchal vision. In what we may call Emily Brontë's mirror-vision, subject and object, self and other, observer and world, male and female, are not necessarily seen as *opposite* in the same way as 'normal' perception detects them to be. Mirror-vision reverses window-vision, so that if we put out the left hand to a mirror, it meets its reflection's right hand; in shaking hands with a friend, right will meet right. '"I *am* Heathcliff"' is mirror-vision; '"I love Linton"' looks out through the norm of the window.

I offer such speculations without dogmatic intent, but rather as a way of mitigating current feminist readings which have the unfortunate (and, I imagine, inadvertent) side-effect of reflecting a weakened and impaired image of the woman poet. It both belittles and falsifies Emily Brontë to present her thus:

> The poet is never confident of her power over language and over imagination because both are, to her, alien and masculine, therefore dangerous to the self's integrity . . . In the poems the poet is obliged, unwillingly, to value possession positively by characterising it as transcendence.[27]

Can this troubled, riven, uncertain figure really be intended to equate with the Emily Brontë whose aggressive and authoritative voice speaks 'No coward

15

soul', 'Riches I hold in light esteem'? We know Emily
Brontë's voice specifically for its power. We may
contrast the straight-line efficiency and drive of her
poetic voice with the frequent querulous compromises
of Wordsworth and Coleridge concealing an uncertain
sense of identity in a fog of verbosity: the double
negatives, pompous circumlocutions and Miltonisms,
the nervous search to hide in mother nature's volumi-
nous skirts. In Emily Brontë's ruthless economy of
articulation lies the brag of freedom. Registering the
vigour in that voice, it is hard to comprehend why a critic
would theorise on its enfeeblement. Emily Brontë's
disputes with her daemonic possessor (her male Muse,
considered by Homans to be experienced as destructively extrinsic to the poet's identity) are conducted in a
voice of powerful and positive synthesis. Here, Freudian
psychoanalysis of the text is talkatively drowning out
the reality of Emily Brontë's characteristic rhythmic
forcefulness; and it seems generally true to say that the
criticism of the later 1970's and '80's tends to declare the
contemporary dark sense of fissure within our present
culture, rather than attending to qualities of voice.
Jungian terms of reference—because they are rooted
in symbolic discourse of poetry and myth—ought ideally
to take more sensitive account of Emily Brontë's
striving for integration of *animus* and *anima* figures
within the text of poetry and novel. As yet, however,
this has not been the case, because of the tendency to
psychoanalyse the author through the novel, which is
in literary terms a dead end, and because of critics'
failure to address tonality and inflection of language
as the measure of meaning, in favour of floating
generalisations: 'Wuthering Heights is a pure, androgynous
novel' (Heilbrun); Emily's poems 'prove a deep journey
into the unconscious' (Hannah).[28]

16

Another symptom of the unease of current feminist trends lies in the reading of Milton as the bane of the female imagination. Two misreadings come to mind, exemplary because they typify modern positions about gender which we need to reassess. Firstly, critics have attributed to Milton statements which he never made, presumably because they assume or wish that he had, as conveniently demonstrating a formula of misogyny: 'God deprives Eve of her dignity by not speaking to her directly, with the result that Milton can say that she prefers to listen only to Adam, "not capable her ear/Of what was high"' (*Paradise Lost* [*PL*] VIII. 49–50).[29] It is to be imagined that nineteenth-century women authors knew Milton better than the twentieth-century critic. The passage in question concerns the address of Raphael not of God, and its intent is precisely the opposite of that alleged:

> Yet went she not, as not with such discourse
> Delighted, or not capable her ear
> Of what was high: such pleasure she reserved,
> Adam relating, she sole auditress...
>
> (VIII.48–51)

Milton goes out of his way to insist that Eve *is* capable of high discourse: but she has sat through the two-and-a-half books of Raphael's exposition of the War in Heaven and the Creation, the plants need watering and the narrator must evacuate her so that Raphael and Adam can discuss her. For these reasons she is permitted to skip the rest of the lecture. A second fallacy imputes an immunity to the male poet (again typified by Milton) from the threatening dominance of his female Muse, whereas the female poet is said to exhibit anxiety before the male supremacy of hers.[30] But Milton's invocatory descriptions of the state of possession, where terror and joy are conjoint, and proximate to death (since consciousness is shed with control),[31] are in practice far more agonised than anything in Emily Brontë's poetry. Precisely because of the duteous allegiance the male poet must show to the father-culture—and, in the case of Milton, as a function of the lifelong conflict between obedience to his own father, internalised as an authority-figure, and his own revolutionary energies as son—he cannot squeeze through the needle's eye to liberty through which an anarchic daughter, unburdened by the freight of caste, might deftly slip.

The present work treats Emily Brontë's singular vision as an extreme development of Radical Protestantism: perhaps the most extreme version in our language, which maintains the inheritance of the Bible—Father-God, Heaven–Earth–Hell, Lucifer, Genesis, the Fall—solely in order to protest it back against itself. *Wuthering Heights* opposes and reverses scriptural revelation as mirrors reverse images, with exactitude. It answers back. The novel is a sublime act of filial, literary and religious disobedience. It presents a child's-eye-view of Scripture, specifically, a girl-child's. The work mocks God and his angels; it derides the godly community. It reverses scriptural values, elevating mortal woman above God, and the creation above the Creator. Mother precedes father. Woman is a law unto herself. The power to make this judgment resides within the Protestant tradition itself, and Emily Brontë is Milton's legitimate daughter in the sense that she inherits not only that individualism with which he opposed one after another *all* the significant majority groupings of his day, ecclesiastical and political, but also the characteristically Miltonic dynamic impulse to forge a re-created world in his own revolutionary image (which for her would be female as well as heterodox).

The tradition of dissenting Protestantism inherited by Emily Brontë and her sisters contains within itself a powerful dualism: both the repressive Calvinism, whose shadow on their lives was cast by the Cornish Calvinistic Methodism of Aunt Branwell (quite distinct from the gracious Arminianism of the mainstream Methodist tradition) and the liberationism of that Protestant individualistic, democratic and inspirationist spirit which has been the heart's blood of English Radicalism. This polarity is a—perhaps, *the*—central dynamic of religious energy in *Wuthering Heights*. Judged as an example of saturnalian reversal, the novel presents itself as an act of literary sedition of the utmost rascality on the one hand and the gravest religious seriousness on the other. It partakes of the spirit of English revolutionary Puritanism in its priest- and church-hating zeal; its vendetta against the self-advertising godly man; its glorifying of the intensely singular vision, and its authorisation of the questioning of all matters of faith, including the status and location of Heaven and Hell, the fact of the Fall and the goodness of God. The very comedy of *Wuthering Heights*—a scathing and irate mockery of orthodoxy and pious pretension—is true to the traditions of Puritan satire. Humour in the novel is a response in kind to God's bad joke: the Creation. It lashes back against her Calvinist inheritance as a kind of damnably black humour and an offence to suffering humanity. To reject the God of Rejection (see pp. 126–46 below), the novel lays hold of the energies unleashed by the liberationist tides of Protestantism which constituted the other half of Emily Brontë's religious inheritance, whose revolutionary implications so far as English history is concerned have been unforgettably described for us by Tawney and Christopher Hill.[32] To read the iconoclasm of *Wuthering Heights* in a seventeenth century alignment, when these features of Protestantism surfaced into a language of heretical reversal, yields an oddly clarifying perspective:

> Oh, these are the men that would turn the world upside down, that make the nation full of tumults and uproars, that work all the disturbance in church and state.

> Freedom is the man that will turn the world upside down, therefore no wonder he hath enemies.[33]

The attitudes struck by *Wuthering Heights* which still have power to shock its readers—the central protagonists' relocation of Heaven as an earthly sanctuary; their disavowal of allegiance to the paternity of God; their refusal of the church and their rejection of the reality of sin (see pp. 146–50 below)—are all logical extensions of certain features of Protestant thought, and familiar in Levelling Puritanism. Milton's dismissal of 'imaginary and scarcrow sins',[34] the Ranter conviction that sin exists only in the imagination, the Quaker belief in the sacred duty of interrupting church services and haranguing the minister[35] (see p. 130–2 below), Winstanley's internalisation and secularisation of Heaven and Hell ('what you call the devil is within you. . . . Every Saint is a true Heaven')[36] his belief in universal salvation,[37] his Pantheism and his belief in the primacy of the inner law and voice for 'every man *and woman*' (emphasis added)[38] with their duty to declare their personal truth, however heretical, have obvious relevance for the reading of *Wuthering Heights* as an extreme Protestant document before it is a late Romantic text. It draws on Protestant energies to desacralise institutionalised Protestantism. Emily Brontë, we know, ceased to attend church. As the daughter of a Church of England priest she vacated the House both of her God and her father. In making this withdrawal she was acting not only within the Protestant tradition of honouring the dictates of inner conviction (comparably with George Eliot in her 'holy war' with her Evangelical father)[39] but in a manner genuinely Miltonic, for Milton too in his latter years narrowed down his personal Church to a community of one.[40] The confidence to turn the world inside-out and upside-down—to make the self into the world, by sucking into its inner cosmos all value and meaning, standing to society in a misfit's role of self-vindicating extrusion—stems in each from belief in an inner light which eclipses all variant realities. Emily Brontë's few recorded remarks to outsiders bear the mark of the Protestant spirit of spiritual self-reliance. 'I wish to be as God made me', she tells the schoolgirls at Brussels who deride her outlandish appearance. 'That's right', is her sole contribution to a discussion in which Mary Taylor has observed that one's religion is entirely a personal matter.[41] Likewise, the flat dismissal of all counter-theologies in the lyric 'No coward soul' shares the Puritan zeal of a latter-day Ecclesiastes:

> Vain are the thousand creeds
> That move men's hearts, unutterably vain,
> Worthless as withered weeds
> Or idlest froth amid the boundless main
>
> To waken doubt...
>
> (ll. 9–13)

The Protestant focus upon the insignificance of externals becomes in Emily Brontë an heroic fanaticism which affirms the value of the private self as sacred inner space, the sanctuary of illumination. To the plenitude of that guarded inwardness is attributed the power and prestige

of an ungendered, unlimited state of being, corresponding with the state of Grace. The interiority of Emily
Brontë's vision, together with the figuring of the inner
world as a sanctuary (the temple of the Spirit), often
remembers Milton:

> though fallen on evil days,
> On evil days though fallen, and evil tongues;
> In darkness, and with dangers compassed round,
> And solitude; yet not alone ...
>
> *(PL* VII.25-8)

> What matters it that all around
> Danger and grief and darkness lie ...
> ('To Imagination', 13-14)

For Emily Brontë as for Milton, the Spirit/Muse is
identified with comfort ('The Holy Spirit, the Com-
forter'): he is 'sure solacer of human cares' (l. 35) and,
in 'O thy bright eyes' he is 'my advocate' (l. 8), alluding
to the Holy Ghost as Paraclete sent by God to plead
man's case against the Old Law.[42] But according
to Emily's lifelong practice of reversal, as the figure of
her Muse develops through her poetry and metamor-
phoses into the Heathcliff of *Wuthering Heights*, he turns
to defend the apostate self against a God who cannot be
perceived as a friend. It is this power to think and write
as *Eikonoklastes*, which is reinforced by the Miltonic spirit,
regardless of the peculiarities of the personal misogyny
from which Milton himself seems to have suffered so
uncontrollably. Like him, she takes up a strong-willed,
intolerant posture of resistance to fruitless external
influence, including his own legacy of anti-feminist
mythography. She pockets what she chooses from the
traditions of the fathers, and like a thief in the night
closes her own doors behind her against intrusion.

Introduction

By making this raid on the Miltonic material, Emily
Brontë is able to steal the passionate religious energies
that make her novel appear the embodiment of a myth.
One may read it alongside Genesis, or Plato's myth of
the spherical two-in-one people cloven for their rebellion against Zeus in the *Symposium* as a story of
originations. Along with these myths of creation, it is
equally a story about (and partial explanation of)
punishment, loss and pain. The work is permeated, as
critics were not slow to realise, with sadism and
brutality: violent conflict is a quality of the world the
characters inhabit. As an aspect of character, it is related
to the sense of rejection or usurpation which universally
afflicts the people of her novel. This apprehension of
man as a wandering outsider which haunts Emily
Brontë's work stems, as we have seen, from her own
posture as an outsider, extrinsic to norms of perception
(something like Heathcliff the 'out-and-outer' peering in
through the window at society [p. 47]), and from her
deduction of a rationale for personal heresy from the
inner logic of Protestantism. During adolescence, she
added the inheritance of Romanticism, and especially
that of Byron whom her imagination seems to have
greeted as a brother, whose attack on God, elevation of
sibling-love and deification of maternal nature reinforced her inverted structuring of Christian myth. Of
the poets whose influence Emily Brontë seized, Byron
represents an exception to her practice of total
submergence of sources within the opacities of her
narrative style (see pp. 5–9 above). Vestiges of Byron are
perceptible at crucial and related moments (see above,
pp. 7–8) rippling the surface of the text with the hint of
clues to total meaning. However, Byron never seems to
have elicited 'anxiety of influence' in Emily Brontë, to
whom he may have appeared less as a mastering

authority than as a brother with whom to identify: it is significant that her special debt to Byron manifests itself in terms of his treatment of brother–sister love as a holy bond in an unholy world. *Cain* and the 'Mystery Plays' proposed to her imagination a way of rereading both Scripture and Milton which would yield a language of indictment against the God whose judgement on Eve made all human children rejects from their first home in Eden. In both authors, accursed humanity seems to exclaim all together, with Cain, 'My punishment is greater than I can bear' (Genesis 4 : 13). Man as 'a fugitive and vagabond . . . in the earth' (4 : 12) calls upon God to account to humanity, or forfeit his children's allegiance in favour of their bond to one another within the matrix of the equally fallen and condemned mother-world.

The theme of the rejected child in *Wuthering Heights* incorporates the language of reprobation as a reproof and challenge to the Creator. On a naturalistic level, rejection in childhood is the emotional centre of the novel, and the present work takes as its initial focus the task of encountering the texture of *Wuthering Heights* as a kind of forcefield of primal linguistic energy: its rhythms, gestures and obsessive patterns of utterance seeming to reproduce on the page a version of child-speech more nakedly authentic than fiction has generally known how to spell out. Close textual analysis of *Wuthering Heights* (notoriously so difficult to achieve in this allegedly 'closed book') is an essential basis for clarification of the obscurities both of religious implication and the semantics of gender within the novel. Both, I think, are rooted in the activation and animation of a version of child-perception on the part of the characters and within the narrative articulation of character and action. *Wuthering Heights*, it has been said, 'is not on the

Child orientated novel

side of "maturity"'.[43] This is an understatement. The novel galvanises our sympathies toward anarchy, disobedience, pagan joy: its protagonists' aversion to the codes of evasion and restriction of adult and civilised life is seductive and winning. The reader is magnetised by Catherine's and Heathcliff's dash for home in the androgynous vision of childhood. In recreating this vision, the novel censures the gender-categories of the adult world; adolescent rebellion against the codes of the elders becomes, in terms of the novel's religious concerns, a cosmic rejection of the accepted (and, in Emily Brontë's day, assumed) creed of the Father-God, the priesthood of her own father and his church.

Uniquely among mythopoeic works of fiction, *Wuthering Heights* raises the mother-principle (projected as the earth, the traditional *terra mater*) to the status of deity, presenting it as the focal object of human aspiration and the final end of Emily Brontë's language of desire. I have suggested this elsewhere,[44] but I will here more fully argue the evidence for believing that *Wuthering Heights* (which on this as on every other issue of authorial opinion holds its peace, never mentioning the earth as 'mother' nor concerning itself with nature goddesses) is predicated on this archetype. Such testimony is fairly abundant—both Charlotte's account of her sister's nature-religion, and the internal evidence of Emily Brontë's poems and essays—but its status needs to be assessed.

When Emily died, Charlotte was busy about the borders of her poetry, commenting, moralising, glossing, adding stanzas of her own, and editing words and phrases. This grief-stricken exercise has a twofold object: to make coherent the meanings of her sister's work and to forge her own communication across the abyss of final departure with a genius which she had both understood and crucially failed to understand. After 'Aye there it is!' which closes:

> Thus truly when that breast is cold
> Thy prisoned soul shall rise,
> The dungeon mingle with the mould—
> The captive with the skies

Charlotte responds:

> Nature's deep being, thine shall hold,
> Her spirit all thy spirit fold,
>   Her breath absorb thy sighs.
> Mortal! though soon life's tale is told,
> Who once lives, never dies![45]

Repeating the rhyme-sounds of Emily's last stanza, Charlotte typically overruns the form with her looser inflection and vaguer, clichéed diction. The stanza conveys a sad bravado, which fails to capture the thrust of Emily's invigorated assertion of the 'principle' of life she intuits under the stress of the wind, and substitutes a far more anthropomorphic image of mother nature sighing her offspring back into her cradling maternity. Charlotte's last two lines are rhetorically noisy and hortatory, but proverbial and empty. The profound solace offered by Emily's poetry comes—strangely—of the impersonality of its animistic 'Mother nature', who, elemental and inhuman, sings no lullaby and rocks no cradles. In this poem, earth takes the remains of the body, and the wind takes the spirit, by force. Emily's imagery, in her powerfully verb-founded language, is of awakening (*kindled, swept, dashed, pouring*); Charlotte's is soporific. What Charlotte does in this marginal addendum (rocking her own pain in her own arms) is precisely to reverse her sister's meaning, so that Emily's drive for liberation in the anonymity of a universe intellectually abstracted to contending 'influence', 'principles', becomes Charlotte's desire to enclose (*hold, fold*) the whole of the lost mortal in peace and quiet. Emily's poem ends in division: body and soul part company, each taking two alternate lines to enact their schism. Charlotte's conclusion is a message dropped back into the past, as if such words could conjure her sister into having 'never died' and thus rouse her into consciousness to read such affirmation.

The marginalia to Emily's poems adequately exemplify the problem of obtaining insight through Charlotte as a medium. The rationalising and expository tendency of her mind contradicts Emily's guarded utterance. Yet her marginalia, letters and the Emily she regenerates as the heroine of *Shirley*[46] communicate her genuine excitement, curiosity and anxiety about Emily's meanings together with a degree of experience and loving insight unparalleled in any other observer. Charlotte's activities in relation to Emily's creativity resemble those of a Renaissance mythographer relaying the original pagan myths to his own generation, covered in accretions of anachronistic exegesis, annotation and Christian rationalisation of the intransigent and self-reflexive narrative material. Charlotte, of course, was a Church of England Protestant of a militant sort, the true child of the Reverend Brontë, carrying her own superb eccentricities of principle and persuasion within a theological perspective that was in the end securely traditional. But Charlotte, too, had been subject to the Calvinist influence which so afflicted Anne and provoked Emily into her own free-thinking imaginings of election and damnation. *Jane Eyre* is an example of the Puritan spirit at its most libertarian, egalitarian and socially radical. Jane's pilgrimage from the outer darkness of exclusion at Gateshead to the eventual Grace of Ferndene presents a humane Revelation of a new heaven *in* a new earth, not foreign to the more spectacular heresies of *Wuthering Heights*.[47] *Jane Eyre* also comprehends the principle of the feminine within the span of Deity: the intercessive lunar figure who counsels the orphaned heroine;[48] more especially, the archetype of the mother-within-the-moors which Jane's journey through the wilderness invokes, in a prose whose biblical periods and Bunyanesque sweetness and rigour command respect for a Christian pantheism of a most unusual sort:

> I touched the heath: it was dry, and yet warm with the heat of the summer day. I looked at the sky; it was pure: a kindly star twinkled just above the chasm ridge. The dew fell, but with a propitious softness; no breeze whispered. Nature seemed to me benign and good; I thought she loved me, outcast as I was; and I, who from man could anticipate only mistrust, rejection, insult, clung to her with filial fondness. To-night, at least, I would be her guest, as I was her child: my mother would lodge me without money and without price. I had one morsel of bread yet. . . . I saw ripe bilberries gleaming here and there, like jet beads in the heath: I gathered a handful, and ate them with the bread. (p. 350)

The moor is the wilderness of Exodus; the dew which comes with such clemency to the tinder-dry heath falls as it fell to the refugees from Egyptian tyranny, as succour from the Provider:

> and in the morning the dew lay round about the host.
>   And when the dew that lay was gone up, behold, upon the face of the wilderness there lay a small round thing, as small as the hoar frost on the ground.
>   And when the children of Israel saw it, they said to one another, It is manna (Exodus 16:13–15)

But the moor is also, recognisably, Haworth Moor, to which both Charlotte and Emily had clung from childhood 'with filial fondness'. This is a statement of affiliation to 'my mother', and an acceptance not simply of the all-providing Father's charity in manna but also of communion with the mother-world: the bread Jane brings with her, the crimson wine of the bilberries. The feminisation of the myth occurs, of course, within a Christian devotional framework (the night-sky for Charlotte, as never for Emily, signifies 'His infinitude, His omnipotence, His omnipresence' [p. 351]) but the consigning of the needy soul and body to source occurs as a 'burial' in the protective heather (p. 350), a 'nestl(ing) to the breast of the hill' (p. 351). The immediacy of the mother-world presents a sanctuary for the pilgrim whose Father displays his power in remote abstractions, not milk but the Milky Way, a colossal system of stars. In her depiction of the 'golden desert' of 'this spreading moor' as a home-world to man (more properly, woman) the refugee, Charlotte Brontë records—in a style of rigorously simple beauty ('I touched . . . I looked . . . I thought . . . I saw . . . and ate')—a religious vision experienced in common with Emily, rendered in tough, plain English and grown from the identical root of familial experience. Charlotte was hence in a unique position to understand Emily's conceptions, at least in this earlier period.

In *Shirley*, Charlotte Brontë offers a discussion between the two heroines, Shirley and Caroline, concerning Genesis and its relation to the Christian Church, to Milton and to mother nature, and the place of woman in the creation. This is a key discussion in trying to guess out whatever religious beliefs might have animated Emily Brontë and shaped *Wuthering Heights*. We cannot, of course, take any of what is said and done in this chapter on trust as literal evidence by which to assess Emily Brontë. _Shirley_ is a fiction, not a biography or documentary record. And this is Charlotte Brontë's Emily, her rough edges and truculent audacity of mind softened to become more palatable to the author and the imagined readership. Shirley is Emily rendered as a survivor: rich, powerful, eligible and married to a happy ending, finally and willingly mastered and accommodated within society. So it is likely to be Emily conventionalised and moralised. The chance to verbalise Emily's beliefs for her must inevitably imply a remedial control of Emily through manipulation of her nature in the mesh of Charlotte's own (always highly polemical) language. Charlotte's Emily is likely to appear radical rather than revolutionary. As against this, there is Charlotte's endeared and awed respect for the spartan beauty of her sister's character; her own habits of artistic realism as a pledge and obligation of her pen; her wish to perpetuate a recognisable and authentic image of Emily into future time. In Chapter 18 Charlotte presents a confrontation between the Miltonic Eve and 'Jehovah's daughter'.[49]

The dialogue between Shirley and Caroline begins with Shirley's refusal to enter the church into which the 'multitudes' are gathered (p. 358), despite the fact that, as Caroline timidly observes, 'my uncle will be angry, if he observes our absence' (p. 358). The discussion which ensues quickly becomes a feminist critique of male religious traditions, taking Milton as their spokesman and authority, as a latter-day patristic interpreter of Scripture. Shirley equates Nature (in an intercessive posture, 'praying for a fair night' with Eve, the source of the human race and the original of its virtues, energies, fortitude and redemptive capacities. Charlotte's reproduction of the diction of the visionary Emily Brontë is a mannered and Latinate 'high style' foreign to the Anglo-Saxon brevity of Emily's characteristic mode of address:

> 'I see her. . . . she is like what Eve was when she and Adam stood alone on earth.'
> 'And that is not Milton's Eve, Shirley.'
> 'Milton's Eve! Milton's Eve! I repeat. No, by the pure Mother of God, it is not! Cary, we are alone: we may speak what we think. Milton was great; but was he good? His brain was right; how was his heart? . . . Angels serried before him their battalions; the long lines of adamantine shields flashed back on his blind eyeballs the unutterable splendor of heaven. . . . Milton tried to see the first woman; but, Cary, he saw her not. . . .
> 'It was his cook that he saw; or it was Mrs Gill, as I have seen her, making custards, in the heat of summer, in the cool dairy, with rose-trees and nasturtiums about the latticed window, preparing a cold collation for the Rectors—preserves and "dulcet creams" . . . .' (p. 359)

There is a certain grotesque disparity between the (one must presume) fully clothed and elderly Mrs Gill bustling at the window and the magnificent nudity of Milton's Eve, from which the author averts her maidenly eyes. Shirley's objection is not at all to the maternal role of Milton's Eve but to the poet's domestication of woman as an original servant-class in the household of Eden. Shirley's feeling for Eve as the archetype of the Great Mother and the personification of natural creativity is in fact perfectly attuned to Miltonic feeling. *Paradise Lost* everywhere declares itself in awe of Eve as the source of human nature and history:

> 'Whence hail to thee,
> Eve rightly called mother of all mankind,
> Mother of all things living, since by thee
> Man is to live, and all things live for man.'
>
> (*PL* XI: 158–61)

Adam's salutation of the now fallen Eve—'"Mother...
Mother"' acknowledges her primary status as the
agency through which all human attainment is made
possible. Charlotte Brontë's Shirley objects to Milton's
tendency to demythologise and denaturalise the archetype of the Great Mother: the culinary Eve preparing a
cold meal for her master in Eden is not just reduced into a
servant class but removed from the 'raw' state of natural
creativity which generates all the power in the archetype
into the closed world of culture and its artificial mingling
of elements for human exploitation. 'Milton's cook' and
great creating Nature oppose each other as society does
the wilderness. Shirley's oath, 'No, by the pure Mother of
God...!' resonates oddly—as an essentially Catholic
phrase—in the midst of Charlotte Brontë's Protestant
eloquence. It momentarily angles at us the wayward
notion familiar to most thinking children that the male
Deity must logically have had a female antecedent.
Shirley's doctrine of nature subliminally presses toward
the heresy of the priority of the female to the male. As a
source rather than a derivative, the female is God's
covert superior and his potential adversary. However,
Charlotte reduces the shock-value in the heresy her
narrative mediates, by casting before it a smokescreen of
archaic classical humanism, disclosing Emily's unortho-
doxies through the canny device of obfuscation. The
appeal to classical mythology is itself profoundly anti-
Miltonic: Milton severely censures such allusion in
Paradise Lost: 'Not the fair field/Of Enna' (IV:268-9), 'thus
they relate,/Erring' (I:746-7; emphasis added):

> 'I would beg to remind him that the first men of the earth
> were Titans, and that Eve was their mother; from
> her sprang Saturn, Hyperion, Oceanus; she bore
> Prometheus—'

'Pagan that you are! What does that signify?'

'I say, there were giants on the earth in those days: giants that strove to scale heaven. The first woman's breast that heaved with life on this world yielded the daring that could contend with Omnipotence: the strength which could bear a thousand years of bondage,—the vitality that could feed that vulture death through uncounted ages,—the unexhausted life and uncorrupted excellence, sisters to immortality which, after milenniums of crimes, struggles, and woes, could conceive and bring forth a Messiah. The first woman was heaven-born....' (pp. 359–60)

This outburst of classicism, somewhat deflated (or authorially neutralised) by the ironically commonsensical Caroline as 'a hash of Scripture and mythology', challenges authority both in its humanistic and allegorising willingness to collapse Christian truth into pagan legend and in its simultaneous elevation of mythology into spiritual truth. Eve, allegorised as the primordial goddess Earth (Gaia) is remembered as the bearer of children inveterately antagonistic to their father ('from her sprang Saturn, Hyperion, Oceanus'); and the feeling in the original narratives is reciprocal, for—as Hesiod tells us—'these most awful sons of Earth and Heaven/ Were hated by their father from the first'.[50] Hence, the feminist mythology attributed by Charlotte Brontë to Shirley/Emily incorporates a vehement objection to the Father, comparable with that expressed by Byron's Cain as he protests against the ruthlessness of the Creation in general (the Father-God) and his own birth in particular (the father Adam):

Cursed be
He who invented life that leads to death!
Or the dull mass of life, that, being life,
Could not retain, but needs must forfeit it—

Even for the innocent!
Lucifer. Dost thou curse thy father?
Cain. Cursed he not me in giving me my birth?
(*Cain*, II.ii.18–23)[51]

Shirley points to the profound antagonism between the Father and his sons, in a manner that the struggle between the males in *Wuthering Heights* seeking power at the Heights (the 'H' coded characters, Hindley, Heathcliff, Hareton) also exemplifies.

Shirley's digression from Scripture to classical mythology reveals a spirit proudly Babylonian and Satanic, through which Eve's energy realises itself in the enmity of generations of her children as they struggle up against the conditions of their creation. Hence Eve is revealed as the revolutionary original of all acts of filial disobedience, which are valued as the thrust of upstanding virtue rather than subjected to reproof.

The most significant of Eve's named children from the point of view of identifying the character of this virtue is Prometheus. Shirley's Aeschylean and especially Shelleyan spirit venerates the 'daring which could contend with Omnipotence' and entertain a mediatorial role between Earth and Heaven, not by transmitting the overflow of divine love to earth but by resistance to divine tyranny: the transmission of stolen fire and the assumption of the punitive wrath of the Father to himself. By insinuating classical mythology into Scripture, Shirley displays a curiously archaic process of reasoning reminiscent of the sleights of Renaissance humanistic syncretism, by means of which she cunningly elides Christian 'Truth' with classical 'fable', pretending to an allegorical relationship between the two which is all gesture and no substance. Caroline, speaking up for Charlotte's robust orthodoxy against this challenge to tradition, is properly shocked: '"Pagan that you are!

What does that signify?"' Shirley is denying the fall. For original sin, she substitutes original virtue. In covertly conflating Jahweh with Zeus, she establishes God as man's natural enemy, against whom it is a human duty to rebel.[52] Promethean woman (projected as Mother Earth) is God's original adversary, but also the agent of redemption to humanity from its servitude. Her 'conception' of an antidote to the Paternal evil ('the Messiah') suggests both a literal and a metaphorical application: the final fruits of stolen knowledge in feminine creation and creativity.

The 'visionary personification of Stilbro' Moor as a 'woman-Titan' which concludes the episode shows Charlotte Brontë attempting to close the breach between God and woman which the excursion into classical mythology had opened wide:

> 'she reclines her bosom on the ridge of Stilbro' Moor; her mighty hands are joined beneath it. So kneeling, face to face she speaks with God. That Eve is Jehovah's daughter, as Adam was his son.'
>
> 'She is very vague and visionary. Come, Shirley, we ought to go into church.'
>
> 'Caroline, I will not: I will stay out here with my mother Eve, in these days called Nature...' (p. 361)

Mother of Prometheus; daughter of Jehovah; vast enough to look God full in the face *as she kneels* (what if she stood up?): Charlotte Brontë's version of Emily's Mother Nature is a curious composite of classical and scriptural, piety and pride. If, as Mrs Gaskell reported, Charlotte partly intended Shirley to represent Emily as she might have been 'had she been placed in health and prosperity',[53] we need—in order to distil from this conversation any inference about Emily's beliefs—to dissolve the authentic memories from the accretion of

Charlotte's stylistic mannerisms and interpretative principles. Doubtless, any conclusions will be conjectural, but several suggestions seem justifiable. First Emily had refused allegiance to the Christian religion as authorised by the Church, in favour of a religion of nature, which she associated with the feminine in general, and the mother-principle in particular. She had a Promethean relish for religious struggle, being as pugilistic as her brother Branwell in her own way, seldom being known in her personal life to lose the opportunity for a just fight. I shall try to show the fierce joy with which *Wuthering Heights* (that war of words) enacts the tussle with the Almighty (see pp. 62–3 below). Second, we can deduce from *Shirley* the fact that Emily had strong feelings about Milton, both of excitement and antipathy, which she was fond of airing in private, taking issue with his conception of Eve as the weak point in *Paradise Lost*. She knew *Paradise Lost* very well. Third, Emily's perception of nature, to judge from *Wuthering Heights* and the poems, was undoubtedly very *unlike* the anthropomorphic, humanitarian and pietistic one presented by Charlotte in *Shirley*. There seems little doubt that the novel's classicising of its heroine's beliefs is a way of translating them out of the blunt English in terms of which Emily would have spelt out her private code, into a parlance familiar but safely foreign and antiquated.

To find an English version we have only to turn to the corpus of Emily Brontë's lyric poetry. Here the search for liberty and peace is consistently associated with the sanctuary of a moorland vista, the nocturnal dream-world traditionally allied with the feminine, and with the more threatening but ultimately benign realm of the underworld in its ancient treaty and concord with the upper world (figured in the Persephone/Demeter myth,

which has been shown to shape so many nineteenth
century novels by women, including, to some degree,
Wuthering Heights).[54] The pull of earth invariably disen-
chants her poetic personae with the allure of heaven, to
such a degree as to arrest allegiance at source. Here I
shall look closely at one of the most telling of the lyrics, 'I
see around me tombstones grey', where the persona
names as *mother* the archetypal affinity which binds her
to earth and the mother-religion. Acknowledging the
unhealing pain of terrestrial life, she analyses it out of
intrinsic connection with heaven:

> Sweet land of light! thy children fair
> Know nought akin to our despair
> . . .
> Well, may they live in extasy
> Their long eternity of joy;
> At least we would not bring them down
> With us to weep, with us to groan.
> No—Earth would wish no other sphere
> To taste her cup of sufferings drear;
> She turns from Heaven a careless eye
> And only mourns that *we* must die!
>
> (ll. 15–16, 21–8)

The immune 'children of heaven' live in a self-absorbed
trance of bliss, narcissistically disconnected from knowledge of their proximity to the incurable and chaotic pain
endured on earth. To know would be to compassionate,
and to feel compassion would be to fall into a share of
pain. The Father's children must be allowed to retain
their hard hearts. The children of Earth (personalised as
'she', hence the children of the Mother) are a race of
implicit moral superiority, who 'would not bring them
down' to fall into human comprehension of pain. Angels
and mortals, as in Byron's mystery play, *Heaven and Earth*,

whose influence I shall assess later (see pp. 94–5) inhabit the poles of a contradictory universe. This poem is a declaration of primary allegiance to the mother-principle, affirming with characteristic hauteur a creation separable from its God and denying the necessity of a contract between them. To deny the fact or desirability of mediation between heaven and earth is by implication to deny Christ. The persona speaks for human nature in refusing to invoke intercession from the Father: 'we would not bring them down/With us to weep'. Such strategic withdrawal from the Divine scheme ironically indicates that human autonomy is essential to preserve the scheme itself intact and pure, contaminating no 'child of heaven' (such as Christ the Son) with the crude matter of human clay. Incarnation and atonement would challenge the perfect polarities upon which the universe is founded. They would indict the Father's logic. The children of the Mother announce their superiority over the refinements of the irrelevantly perfect heaven. From the vantage-point of such elevation, the mother-world can afford to deny the possibility of any redemptive passage or communication between heaven and earth. 'Earth would wish no other sphere/To taste her cup of sufferings drear', remembering—but rebuking—Christ at Gethsemane. Emily Brontë's earth, self-defending in her proud isolation from any bending-down of the intercessive skies, turns a 'careless' eye to heaven and broods inwardly upon her own children. The very existence of memory in human beings makes it impossible that heaven could palliate one's knowledge of bygone pain. The poem emphasises the passionate love-bond between earth and earth's children: it stands as a statement of affiliation, not to the authority of a commanding and omniscient Divine Parent, but to the maternal principle perceived as being *like ourselves* in vulnerability and in staunch commitment to the defence of its young in a world it does not control.[55] Taut abstraction expresses the remote beatitude of the Blessed ('Well, may they live in extasy/Their long eternity of joy'), which is almost metaphysical in its dashingly casual manner. The circle of the octosyllabic couplet closes in half-rhyme, playing a subtle verbal music (*live/long*, *extasy/eternity*) to imply the repetitious circularity of the timeless realm, in which the tautology of '*long* eternity' reflects a possible routine of ennui unknown to the lower world. Earth as *mater dolorosa*, mutely alienated from an unatoning heaven, claims from the speaker a passionately personal affiliation:

> Ah mother, what shall comfort thee
> In all this boundless misery?
>
> (ll. 29–30)

The poetic voice lends its power to articulate the 'deep *unutterable* woe' of the parent planet. For Milton's allegiance to the power and glory of the Father ('Hail, holy Light...') Emily Brontë substitutes an invocation to the earth named as mortal mother. Orphaned of her natural mother since the age of three, she consecrates the earth which contains her dead mother's remains in a poem which declares conscious recognition of the archetypal vision upon which her heretical religion and sinistral perception are founded:

> Indeed, no dazzling land above
> Can cheat thee of thy children's love.
> We all, in life's departing shine,
> Our last dear longings blend with thine;
> And struggle still and strive to trace
> With clouded gaze, thy darling face.

We would not leave our native home
For *any* world beyond the Tomb.
No—rather on thy kindly breast
Let us be laid in lasting rest;
Or waken but to share with thee
A mutual immortality.

(ll. 35–46)

Earth's 'darling face' and 'kindly breast' are loved as human and succouring in a way that the delusive glory of heaven cannot match. Indeed, the radiant children of heaven inhabit a country whose luminous perfection is understood as potential corruption of clear vision. *Dazzle* is an ironic Miltonism, alluding to *Paradise Lost*'s heaven of too intense Light that bears into the surcharged vision of the angel host as a kind of darkness:

Dark with excessive bright thy skirts appear
Yet dazzle heaven, that brightest seraphim
Approach not, but with both wings veil their eyes.

(III:380–2)

To reject transcendence in quintessential Light in favour of immanence within the dying planet is, for the poetic persona, a choice against moral blindness. Fidelity is Emily Brontë's cardinal virtue: both her poetry and fiction are preoccupied with the keeping of faith to one's source and earliest allegiances, if necessary across the boundary of the grave (see pp. 116–9 below). The pledge to the mother-world ('no dazzling world above/Can cheat thee of thy children's love') affirms that mortality's love of its home is faithful as the child to the mother, in wanting to rest its eyes on that face and no other. The eternal reciprocity of shared sleep—featured in *Wuthering Heights* in the shared bed and shared grave of Catherine and Heathcliff, or the (gloriously phrased) 'mutual immortality' of earth with earth's child—is the final focus of desire.

As a self-acknowledged 'child of the Mother', Emily Brontë, as we shall see (pp. 83-8 below) recognises and does not disclaim kinship with the predatory chain of being which characterises nature. But she denies man's and nature's responsibility for their impaired condition, grafting responsibility for the fall on to the God who has unpardonably stigmatised his creation. Her heroine chooses to fall with Lucifer from the reprehensible perfection of the angels back into the world of early affinity: the heath and Heathcliff. My study opens its account of these central themes of *Wuthering Heights* by reflecting on the likeness of the linguistic norms of the novel—apparently so prohibitively opaque—to an original language of childhood desire.

Chapter One

The Language of Familial Desire

Bounded by silences and its own brevity, the life of Emily Brontë addressed itself exclusively inward to the intimate world of its own origins. Beyond the necessary economy of language demanded for practical purposes, she was resolute in confiding words to few outsiders, entering the world minimally, reluctantly, and nearly always with temporarily disastrous consequences to her psyche. She wrote scarcely any letters, left few recorded utterances and never shared herself in friendship.

It is a life, therefore, in which a handful of living figures made up the integrity of a complete cosmos: her father, the Reverend Patrick Brontë, her Aunt Branwell, her brother and sisters Charlotte and Anne, the servant Tabby. Confined together within the restricted space of Haworth Parsonage, these figures revealed the mirroring spectrum of human experience and passion to her, shadowed by the accompanying deaths of the other members of her family: her mother and two elder sisters, Maria and Elizabeth, who had died at the ages of

11 and 10 years. In refusing to entertain the compromise entailed by crossing the threshold from home to society, Emily Brontë preserved and declared in her art a unique integrity. Essentially, her world is the authentic theatre of childhood, interpreted non-commitally into the dialect of the elders (in the narrative voice of her fiction) or transcribed raw on to the page (in the voices of her characters). She makes literate what for most of us is prehistoric: anterior to disclosure and elucidation in the complex, explanatory and modifying composure of written language. The characters of *Wuthering Heights* teem with childhood animosities, allegiances and obsessions; they brawl, taunt, mock, manipulate, weep and play their outdoor and indoor orgiastic games within the vice of a terrible paradox. They are children liberated from the deterrent adult guardians who fence and chasten the outset of human life, but their liberation derives from the conditions that orphan and expose them.[1] Because these beings are versions of children in a child's world, they cannot be judged: the novel's tone is flat and equal, neither knowing nor casting blame or praise. Its insistent edge of asperity seems directed rather at the narrators' effort to interpret and the reader's attempt to participate, the adult voyeurs of the game played by the novel's children. The work guards its borders; it is a domain for private life, like the house at the Heights and the answering house, Thrushcross Grange, each with its different means of seclusion— shut doors and surliness on the one hand, the walled garden on the other.

The novel engrosses itself with the inturned life of family—a family which exerts all its energies upon the reinforcement of its own roots, its own consolidation as an entity in defiance of the dispersals consequent upon existence within the mutable, contingent sphere of

Time. It is deeply concerned with lineage, heredity and patrimony as figures for a kind of retentive change. As the novel's structure is circular, cyclical, so the story of the second generation recapitulates and completes that of the first. The Earnshaw family, by incorporating the agencies of another family, the Lintons, seeks to inbreed into deeper and more speaking reiteration of its own definitive features. Resemblance rather than unlikeness calls out unappeasably for the satisfaction of reunification: the lullaby of solipsism, to conform only to the self. Genealogy[2] is the novel's narrative method of achieving the consolation of a retrenchment of the dispersed seed of being—a new grounding within the original raw material. In the marriage of Catherine II and Hareton, the family goes home to itself. It does so on behalf of the original generation, enacting a myth of becoming—in as literal a way as is viable, short of incest[3]—flesh of one flesh. Catherine and Hareton route the (as it were) transmigrated being of the first Catherine back to destination in source, while her individual body in a parallel process of reunification decomposes into the earth which is equally home and self. Finally, her spirit fuses with the breath which is the moorland wind, wandering out freely upon the sanctuary of her early childhood games.[4] The huge cost paid by the first Catherine in her 'innocent' desire to attain the 'forbidden' world of lost childhood[5]—sacrificial death—is hence mitigated and transformed for the reader by the doubling of plot in her own child's eventual destiny.

Emily Brontë's work commands a unique view of childhood within our literature by exposing a language which hoarded verbatim the values, joys and pains of that state which, if not prelapsarian, presented the fall as an evolutionary sequence of stages of schism, during which process life was entered into with all one's energies in fullest vigour. *Wuthering Heights* charts a series of fractures which will end in that abeyance of vivacity which is the bondage of adult life; but the novel never enters into the language of that experience, and never fully allows its characters to grow up, not to collude in the process. The narrative splits, doubles and multiplies (reiterating names, places, experiences, apparent clues and codes)[6] in a complex and elusive structural pattern of affinity and disparity, with some such curious mathematical unity as we imagine may underlie genetic coding. One of the extraordinary, and unaccountable features of *Wuthering Heights* is the shaping control over such apparently remiss and anarchically childish raw material exerted by an author whose novel seems structured like the codes of DNA. We encounter it like a problem in logic, which, having defeated generations of previous readers, introduces us to a mind forbiddingly outside the *adult* norm, either of male or female artist. Its intellectual vigour and authority invite us to reassess the apparent welter of its 'childish' raw material, as not perhaps so very vagrant: to query, in effect, what good is served by the development of consciousness, education, book-learning itself (major problematic motifs of the novel), those factors, indeed, which led us in the first place to take up *Wuthering Heights* and open it at page 1. The stages of the fall—birth, weaning into consciousness, mother-loss, father-loss, sibling-love and -rivalry, adolescence, marriage, parturition, the final split into a dead self (Catherine I) and its daughter-self—are encountered at every stage with protest by the novel's characters and as a riddle by the narrative voices. Most especially, the value of the adult culture that led to the meeting of author and reader is questioned, most memorably in the voice of Catherine in her final breakdown: '"What in the name of all that feels, has he to do with *books*, when I am dying?"' (p. 122).

It is in the context of this revolutionary questioning of consensus values that we must look at the language of childhood in *Wuthering Heights*. If we examine the qualities of the protagonists' mode of utterance, we can tell from the very timbre of their voices and the manner and mode of their address that even the supposed adults (measuring by years) are only children in disguise.[7] The level of infantilism within their speech-patterns is high. At heart, the novel implies, people don't change; growth is superficial, culture is shallow and easy to erode. Edgar Linton fights his wife for the key to the room, amidst a riot of name-calling, taunts, threats and physical assaults. ' "No, I'll swallow the key before you shall get it!" ' yells Catherine to her magistrate-husband (p 115). In the language of her threat lies the child's spontaneous propensity for outrageous utterance: violent argument is a well-relished game of wills, in which household objects feature as pieces in the game. The infantile patterns of verbal abuse and physical threat, ridiculous as they appear out of context, will nevertheless be recognised as the merest realism by readers familiar with the rhetoric of domestic dissension in the 'real' world outside the novel. When Heathcliff first reappears at Thrushcross Grange, Linton strives to maintain a mincingly fastidious politeness in the face of his rival:

'Catherine, unless we are to have cold tea, please to come to the table. . . .Mr Heathcliff will have a long walk, wherever he may lodge to-night and I'm thirsty.'. . .

The meal hardly endured ten minutes—Catherine's cup was never filled, she could neither eat nor drink. Edgar had made a slop in his saucer, and scarcely swallowed a mouthful. (pp 96–7)

The details noted by the narrator are nursery details: the

petulant '"I'm thirsty"', the slop in the saucer. Like volatile children playing at tea-parties, the protagonists mime a social game as a cover for other games more explosive and disruptive.

The level of disruption achieved by the insanely distressed grown-up children of the novel is attested by the narrator's decision, on occasion, to join in their communal orgy of violence. The huge bid for attention made by the drunken Hindley in his bereavement causes his son Hareton, the 'real' child, to bellow and take refuge in the kitchen cupboard at his uncontrollable parent's approach (p. 73). Hindley's lurid behaviour and utterance have the violent spontaneity and the uncensored rashness and oddity appropriate to a galled infant who acts before he thinks. His towering, incommunicable love for his son issues in the likelihood of Hareton's 'being squeezed and kissed to death'; his fits of rage carry the threat 'of being flung into the fire, or dashed against the wall'. Here the author's characteristically Miltonic, hellfire verbs *flung, dashed,* have the violent, split-second momentum of childlike undirected and non-rational action. The game Nelly plays with Hindley in which she colludes with his behaviour in order to control it, illustrates the narrative's awareness of the register of language and action from which it draws:

'But, with the help of Satan, I shall make you swallow the carving knife, Nelly! You needn't laugh; for I've just crammed Kenneth, head-downmost, in the Blackhorse marsh; and two is the same as one—and I want to kill some of you, I shall have no rest till I do!'

'But I don't like the carving knife, Mr. Hindley,' I answered; 'it has been cutting red herrings—I'd rather be shot, if you please.'

'You'd rather be damned!' he said, 'and so you shall—No

law in England can hinder a man from keeping his house decent, and mine's abominable! open your mouth.'

He held the knife in his hand, and pushed its point between my teeth: but, for my part, I was never much afraid of his vagaries. I spat out, and affirmed it tasted detestably—I would not take it on any account. (p. 73)

The principle of Saturnalia (the local doctor 'head-downmost' in a bog) is a running theme throughout the episode: Hindley swears 'with the help of Satan', his medicinal knife is to be used to purge his lawless household in the name of the 'law in England'. Nelly's answers are ironically obedient to the decorums of the prevailing saturnalian code as she spits it out on account of its unappetising taste. Hindley's murderous 'vagaries' are to her of little more account than the antics of a foster-brother or foster-child, to be managed by humouring and diverting participation. Child's play in the unruly world of the Heights is an expected norm, particularly amongst the adults. Because they have power to convert their extravagant fantasies of revenge and desire into action (Hareton literally dropped by his parent over the banister [p. 74]), these lethal children of the novel insistently menace the control of the narrator who is also a surrogate mother to the group. At the point where the licensed principle of saturnalian misrule threatens to turn the world literally upside down (father kills son), the narrative supplies an ironically remedial presence in the person of their mutual enemy, Heathcliff, who 'by a natural impulse...arrested his descent' (p. 74). Authorial superintendence of the ungovernable antics of the characters takes the form of a practical joke sharing the mode embraced by the unexorcised child-selves of the novel.

Energy is the root of beauty, and the source of energy is the child in us: this is, I think, the unstated aesthetic of *Wuthering Heights*. The first generation of the novel stands most abundantly provided with energy, and hence makes a claim on us and has an attraction for us which subverts all consideration of ethics. The appeal is to the ego of the reader—an ego which has been rigorously starved out and stamped down since childhood, by the very process of education which has ripened the reader into a condition to assess the book. This reversal of moral and cultural norms is a major factor in what I have called Emily Brontë's 'sinistral' structuring of perception (see pp. 12–13 above). The novel calls up and articulates a reader's vestigial nostalgia for the narcissistic mirror-vision of childhood. The ease with which we embrace the unregenerate egos of Catherine and Heathcliff (even, in a different way, Hindley, so recognisably Catherine's kin) indicates our readiness to be seduced back into the pagan hinterland of the mind's past. Amidst the welter of name-calling, fits of affection, dreams and hungers, there is a quality of pure animal vivacity which exerts a powerful pull against the learnt code of adult life which must condemn such impetuosities as anti-social. The urge of the reader is less into sympathy than into identification: 'I *am* Heathcliff' has worked on generations of readers as a personal statement to be made with and through Catherine, though—as if drugged or entranced—one very imperfectly comprehends the meaning of the affirmation. Catherine's beautiful, vagrant speech-patterns are at the centre of the novel aesthetically. They express frank, uncensored outbursts of raw egotism, unmediated by the verbal disguise by means of which we are taught to blur communication of the heart's desires. This unabashed purity of egotism is not only present but intensified at the most holy and awesome moments of the novel, to the degree that it appears to inform the very essence of the novel's value-system. At their last meeting, Heathcliff kneels to embrace Catherine, and as he attempts to rise, she 'seized his hair, and kept him down':

> 'I wish I could hold you ... till we were both dead! I shouldn't
> care what you suffered. I care nothing for your sufferings.
> Why shouldn't you suffer? I do! Will you forget me—will
> you be happy when I am in the earth? Will you say twenty
> years hence, "That's the grave of Catherine Earnshaw. I
> loved her long ago, and was wretched to lose her; but it is
> past. I've loved many others since—my children are dearer
> to me than she was, and, at death, I shall not rejoice that I
> am going to her, I shall be sorry that I must leave them!"
> Will you say so, Heathcliff?' (pp. 158-9)

To elucidate the nature of our complicity and to focus
what Emily Brontë's novel draws our emotions to
endorse, through the uninhibitedly amoral potency of
its heroine's utterance of desire, we may compare it with
her sister Anne's setting of the identical theme (copied,
no doubt, from the same models: Gondal combined with
Branwell's deterioration), in *The Tenant of Wildfell Hall*:

> ' "Death is so terrible," he cried, "I cannot bear it! *You* don't
> know, Helen—you can't imagine what it is, because you
> haven't it before you; and when I'm buried, you'll return to
> your old ways and be as happy as ever, and all the world will
> go on just as busy and merry as if I had never been; while
> I—" He burst into tears.
> ' "You needn't let *that* distress you, " I said; "we shall all
> follow you soon enough."
> ' "I wish to God I could take you with me now!" he
> exclaimed; "you should plead for me."
> ' "No man can deliver his brother...." ' [8]

The scathing pietism of Anne's heroine casting her
sardonic truism at the weeping man (' "You needn't let
that distress you " ') encloses the immediacy of his human
and deeply understandable terrors in the parenthetical

judgement of one whose privilege it is to see constantly from the cold perspective of eternity. Her novel tries to coerce the reader into participation in those terms of judgement, delivered by the female with whom we are requested to identify, against the weak and daunted male. Emily Brontë lifts the speech from any tearful and pitiful context and attributes it to the most powerful and charismatic figure in her novel, where it assumes a lurid grandeur of protest against her own death and against Christian moral standards ('"why shouldn't you suffer? I do!"') Like Huntingdon, Catherine desires to drag her partner down into the grave with her, but her '"I wish I could hold you'" is both more manic and less apologetic than his tamer'" I wish to God I could take you with me"'. Each is willing to exploit and ultimately to sacrifice the existence of the mate, but Huntingdon's (so heavily penalised) desire has at least the rationale of seeking to use Helen as intercessor with the punitive God whose envoy she seems to be; Catherine recognises no God beyond the self. Each imagines a future in which he or she has no part: but Huntingdon's fantasy is abstract and generalised compared with Catherine's. The terms of Catherine's speech indicate a childlike terror of solitude ('being laid alone') conjured up by the hectic and nervous brilliance of her localising imagery: Heathcliff as a doting paterfamilias, ambling past her twenty-year-old grave and delivering himself of a choicely spiteful epitaph is a scenario as fiercely pathetic as it is bazarrely unlikely.

More profoundly, we are moved by Catherine's panic to deeper recognitions of what it is she has to fear. She is hungrily manipulating him, as the wailing claim at the end ('"Will you say so, Heathcliff?"') which craves his contradiction, makes clear. She resembles a child with a horror of being left alone at night; the foundation of her security is threatened. Her fear of being buried alone

while her partner wanders freely about on the face of
things involves, surely, Catherine's terror that *he will
grow up*. 'My children are dearer to me than she was', she
has him say, her fantasy inventing alien children for him
other than herself (his putative wife being no problem
for jealousy, since blood-kin are the authentic objects of
attachment and desire in *Wuthering Heights*. Husbands
and wives are addenda to be accumulated, nobodies,
strangers, necessary for procreation but not germane
and primal). Catherine's hell of fear comes of her new
ability to envisage Heathcliff becoming a member of
another generation, betraying her to an eternity of
childhood atrophied because it is unaccompanied. The
frankness of Catherine's attitude may be tested against
the sophistical generosity practised by the persona in
Shakespeare's sonnet 'No longer mourn for me when I
am dead' (LXXI: 'I in your sweet thoughts would be
forgot,/If thinking on me then should make you woe').
The sonnet fraudulently denies its possessiveness in
order to bait the hooks of possession with merit, by
artistic sleight of hand. The validity of Catherine's claim
on Heathcliff appears more honourable by virtue of its
crude, vindictive honesty. Later, she swerves and
contradicts herself, revealing the deepest sources of her
behaviour as that needy love whose code is the total
allegiance of passionate dependency:

> 'I'm not wishing you greater torment than I have,
> Heathcliff! I only wish us never to be parted—and should a
> word of mine distress you hereafter, think I feel the same
> distress underground, and for my own sake, forgive me!
> Come here and kneel down again! You never harmed me in
> your life. Nay, if you nurse anger, that will be worse to
> remember than my harsh words! Won't you come here
> again? Do!' (p. 159)

The driving motive of Catherine's lifetime is recorded here: *never to be parted.* Union and unanimity of sister- with foster-brother, self with other, male with and in the female, are the ground of being. Catherine's expression of tenderness, exacerbated by her mortal illness, is dictatorial—a reaching through language for power. A cajoling note has crept in—'"Won't you...? Do!"' *Wuthering Heights* is a unique act of search for a language which will capsize the boundaries and thresholds between self and other: a magical language which will somehow empower the creative persona to conjure that dissolution of borders into being; to run time back into itself so that early security and potency may be retrieved. It seeks to recreate the primal condition which is *never to be parted.* In this enterprise, Catherine I is always the central questor for the soul's intimate language to revoke the calamitous laws that disengage one from source. Here she throws up imagery of parallel intuitive sympathies existing in the underworld and above ground ('"should a word of mine distress you...I feel the same distress underground"'). In terms of this fantasy there will be no need for Heathcliff to wake alone; for Catherine to sleep alone. Their severance will simply supply conscious and unconscious versions of one another. Catherine creates bursts of imagery and conceptualisation (of which '"I *am* Heathcliff"' is only the most notably memorable occurrence) for this effort to push language past the barriers of its foundation in a world fragmented and discrete, to do the work of reintegration.

In this work of words, Heathcliff (functioning always as a secondary aspect of Catherine)[9] participates as her double, shadow spokesman or ministering self, reminding her endlessly of the pledge (of integrity with himself) which she has broken. Each time Catherine seeks a formulation which will heal the split—between them; in herself—she fails in her invention, as language does utterly fail to alter the structure of reality. ' "That is not *my* Heathcliff" ', Cathy goes on. ' "I shall . . . take him with me—he's in my soul" ' (p. 160). The strategy now is to internalise a version of the beloved, to take the 'true' (i.e. desired) version into the soul in the guise of a concept and to incorporate him there, leaving the 'false' (i.e. inconvenient) version to his own devices.[10] Now there are two Heathcliffs, an inner and an outer: the effort to unify leads inevitably and ironically in the novel to division and multiplication.[11] Catherine turns away with her preferred version of reality to 'muse' on escape into 'that glorious world' beyond the enclosure of the body; but the extent to which the language's attempt to reconstruct reality dissatisfies and betrays its evanescence and duplicity in the very moment of speech is attested by her restless return to the turned back of Heathcliff: ' "I *wonder* he won't be near me! . . . I thought he wished it. Heathcliff, dear! you should not be sullen now. Do come to me, Heathcliff" ' (p. 160). Turning him into the third person, she mediates her address through Nelly, as sulking infants may be addressed in their pointed self-exile, bargaining for their return. The petulant ' "I *wonder* . . . " ' flounces off into a direct challenge for his obedience to her love, parentally cajoling a child assumed to be corrigible: ' "Heathcliff dear! you should . . . " ' and modulating into that choric refrain which calls between the two from one end of the novel to the other (almost: as Heathcliff fades to a ghostly relict, he ceases to command, moves out to join her): ' "Do come to me, Heathcliff".' From Lockwood's dream-ghost of Cathy: ' "I'm come home" '(p. 23), to Heathcliff's ' "Come in! come in! . . . Cathy, do come. Oh do—" ' (p. 27), to Cathy's ' "I do wish he'd come. I do wish he would" '

(p. 83) after his departure from the Heights, to Heathcliff's delusion of her 'coming in' (p. 290) after her death. The combined pathos and force of this echoing call derives from its being levied as a compulsion upon reality to yield the object of desire to the desirer who (in the very act of utterance) clearly perceives that reality will make no concession to the language of his or her need. The cry apportioned between *come* and *do* has hence the status at once of peremptory demand and of hopeless plea. The cyclical iteration of this phrase (we shall see its Byronic derivation) in the course of the book has an important effect. Its rhythm is the pulse-beat of an absolutely crucial and primary loss beyond which the life of the sufferer cannot develop; or rather, beyond which all development is essentially digressive. The imperative form is at the very edge of language's attempt to invade reality coercively; to force it into the needed shape. As Catherine addresses Heathcliff, ' "Do come to me" ', she herself rises to fling herself toward him, to fulfil on his behalf the appeal of her own words; but this very act of fulfilment is suicidal. Language from this point syllables itself in Catherine's mouth as the pure and unmixed child-speech of extreme desire. It speaks in sentences of two or three words only; it has one point to make, and one only, whose expression it obsessively doubles: ' "Let me alone. Let me alone. . . . If I've done wrong, I'm dying for it. It is enough! You left me too; but I won't upbraid you! I forgive you. Forgive me!" ' (p. 161). *Alone/alone; forgive/Forgive:* the language makes its point by purely echoic devices. It commands; asserts; begs, within the cursory limit of an existence which has (literally) not breath enough left to afford the waste of one word. One final stream of words completes the process whereby the language of naked childhood emotion becomes the soul's last resort in the struggle 'never to be parted':

He would have risen, and unfixed her fingers by the act–she
clung fast, gasping; there was mad resolution in her face.
  'No!' she shrieked. 'Oh, don't, don't go. It is the last time!
Edgar will not hurt us. Heathcliff, I shall die! I shall die!'
(p. 162)

Catherine proclaims the end of the world, in a detaining
volley of negatives: her last word in the novel is *die*, her
final articulate terror is that of separation from
Heathcliff. The detail describing the threat to 'unfix her
fingers' while she 'clung fast' repeats on the narrative
line the burden of the speeches—figuring the will to
claw back time so as to pre-empt change. Catherine's
crisis repeats in another key the theme that obsesses
Emily's poetry: how to keep hold of what we possess,
have possessed, or think we have possessed (for the
moment it finds articulation, possession has already
been lost, or has entered the realm of the problematical).
  In 'How beautiful the earth is still', a poem of 1845
(two years before the publication of *Wuthering Heights*),
the first persona interrogates the second:

> Why dost thou hold the treasure fast
> Of youth's delight, when youth is past
> And thou art near thy prime?
>   (ll. 8–10)

The poem acknowledges and is willing to defend a
retardation of natural growth in order to prolong
indefinitely that life of perpetual expectation proper to
the periods of childhood and adolescence. Imagery of
'treasure' encourages the suggestion of such prorroga-
tion as an act of hoarding, comparable perhaps with
Heathcliff's avaricious accumulation of wealth in
Wuthering Heights. (We may remember that in 1843 Emily
took over the management of her sisters' legacies, and

prided herself on making investments).[12] The poem defends the consciously unfulfilled life as a perpetual fund of anticipation, as against the self-squandering of the 'normal' members of her generation who assent to a world of satiating disappointment. The persona celebrates her retentiveness; the power to 'hold backward from the tempting race':

> 'There cast my anchor of Desire
> Deep in unknown Eternity;
> Nor ever let my Spirit tire
> With looking for *What is to be.*
>
> 'It is Hope's spell that glorifies
> Like youth to my maturer eyes
> All Nature's million mysteries—
> The fearful and the fair—'
>
> (ll. 33–40)

To refuse participation in the communal here-and-now is to seek permanent access to the primitive marvels of life as seen through the child's-eye-view. But to 'cast my anchor of Desire/Deep in unknown Eternity' is to solicit premature death. 'Rewarding Destiny' (with its patently fiscal implication) is Janus-faced. The income on the project of preserving such elation and buoyancy of spirit as characterise early life is plainly (as the poem recognises) not solely a mooring at the haven of source but an anchorage in the home waters of Non-being. Emily's Catherine at this sublime moment of *Wuthering Heights* pays the due exacted by 'Rewarding Destiny' for her passionately self-solacing attachment to the precocious sense of glory founded in her early love of Heathcliff: '"No!...oh don't, don't go....I shall die!"'

The narrative voice intervenes to soothe Heathcliff's perception of Catherine's passage out of the world.

Catherine died '"Quietly as a lamb....as a child reviving"', she tells him (p. 166); having recognised no one after Heathcliff, '"her latest ideas wandered back to pleasant early days"' (p. 167). Nelly as plainly as words can conjure images, seeks to return Catherine to that halcyon interlude which the conscious adult has to die to regain. The child in Catherine is permitted to 'revive' only as the adult dies. Her own child, the new Catherine, is to negotiate with safety the transition from adolescence into adult life: hence the first Catherine is the mother who is displaced by a child and simultaneously the mythic child who must give way to a maturing version of herself. Heathcliff throughout remains static, a fixture to replicate Catherine I's bereavement of herself. The language of search passes to him: '"Where is she? Not *there*—not in heaven—not perished—where?"':

> 'Be with me always—take any form—drive me mad! only *do* not leave me in this abyss, where I cannot find you! O God! it is unutterable! I *cannot* live without my life! I cannot live without my soul!'
> He dashed his head against the knotted trunk (p. 167)

Catherine's release from the turbulent and achingly beautiful language of desire (through disclosure of the new Catherine, the baby who appears to us as a new version of her self, calculated for survival and evolution) casts the burden of that killing language exclusively upon Heathcliff, who receives his inheritance with rage and horror. Language as a commanding and demanding prayer, a speech which derangingly knows its own tight constraints ('"it is unutterable"') descends on Heathcliff like a curse. He localises himself '"in this *abyss*, where I cannot find you "' (emphasis added). Signs, as Hillis Miller has said, in *Wuthering Heights* codify absence, vacancy, no thing.[13] Heathcliff's 'abyss' derives from the *prima materia* from which the Creator–Spirit of Genesis divulged form and meaning, through Milton's 'wild abyss,/The womb of nature and perhaps her grave' (*PL* II.910–11), the abortive 'vast vacuity' (l. 932). Hence he is left stranded in a no-man's-land at once prior to and subsequent to time and space. It is an uncreated world beyond any words, which his language seeks to transform into plenitude by conjuring Catherine to declare her whereabouts. What he resists is her evacuation from reality. He does not resist, rather welcomes, his own pain as a testament to the possibility of her immanence, invoking her to haunt him. The great double assertion which consummates his rage of loss: ' "I *cannot* . . . I *cannot*' " demonstrates the stern literality with which Emily Brontë had contemplated the resources of language: compelling it to stand or fall by the buried metaphors which informed it. The conventional equation of another person with one's own 'life' and 'soul' is accorded by the novel's literalists the status of congruence with human actuality. But in confronting its own self-consistency, this unifying language of mutual identity breaks upon the invincible contradiction offered to it by exterior reality: the loss of Catherine. Hence the passionate repeated negatives—*cannot, cannot*—and the resort of the speaker to an act of expression outside the circumference of words: 'He dashed his head . . . howled, not like a man'. The language of human culture is abject before the confounding 'abyss' of hollowness in the universe to which he is committed. Heathcliff has prayed directly into the abyss and will repeat his prayer 'till my tongue stiffens', that this vast vacuity should yield up a semblance of the desired beloved. The perception that the prayer is unanswerable by the voiceless world beyond the ego is the signal for his human voice to respond by adjusting its form to the formlessness of the Abyss: to collapse into howls for what cannot be found, as the child howls for its mother in the night, *infans*, languageless. Heathcliff nowhere more profoundly than in this passage of degenerating grief incarnates a central theme of the novel—the orphaning of God's child as a cast-off in the universe.

Heathcliff's displays of spectacular excess (bruising Catherine's skin with his grip, 'grinding his teeth' [p. 160], gnashing, foaming, dashing his head against the tree [p. 167]) may be read less as extensions of Gothic convention than as the frantically untempered and inchoate reflexes of childhood.[14] Throughout its first half the novel structures itself as an escalation of uncontrolled tantrum on the part of the central protagonists, Catherine, Heathcliff, Hindley and also Edgar and Isabella Linton (whose family opposition to the children of the Heights is in some sense a spurious one, a less volcanic but equally sincere selfishness).[15] Catherine's death-scene is only one such explosion; Isabella's narrative of the communal degeneration of Hindley-Heathcliff-Isabella at the Heights in Volume 2, Chapter 3, is another (see pp. 143-5 below). The staple mode of address in the novel is that of quarrel, and its structure may be shown to depend upon the evolution of one quarrel out of another, with even the more harmonious or conclusive scenes predicated upon a core of dissent. If Catherine's and Heathcliff's parting (and reconciling) discussion takes the form of a brutal and ruthless struggle of wills, so within each chapter unit action and interest tend to be generated by bad temper, verbal or physical assault, or territorial dispute. Chapter 10 as a sample yields the following structure of argument. Lockwood and Nelly began by arguing over medicine (p. 90), Edgar chides Nelly over the treatment of Catherine (p. 91), Nelly disputes with Heathcliff over his admittance (pp. 92-3), Edgar argues with Catherine over the same thing (pp. 94-5) to which she forces a conclusion by crushing their fingers together (p. 95), Heathcliff addresses Catherine with anger over her marriage (p. 96), Catherine leaves Edgar's bed after a quarrel and abuses him (p. 97), she quarrels with Isabella (pp. 101-3), a dispute which is carried on in front of Heathcliff, Isabella scratching Catherine's cheek (p. 105), and finally Heathcliff abuses Isabella (p. 106). This principle of plot construction as a tightly linked sequence of quarrels typifies in detail the novel's disintegrative tendency as a whole. Within this maelstrom, the peaceful moments seem all the more vulnerable and luminous (within this very chapter, the quiet figures of Catherine and Edgar watching the 'long line of mist winding nearly to [the] top' of the valley of Gimmerton' [p. 93]; the scene in which Edgar puts on Catherine's pillow 'a handful of golden crocuses' [p. 134]). Such peaceful and meditative times are almost always associated with strongly evocative sense of place—place as realising the image of a person long-ago, whether exterior or interior, as for instance when Nelly broods on the neatness of her kitchen—'I smelt the rich scent of the heating spices; and admired the shining kitchen utensils, the polished clock, decked in holly, the silver mugs ranged on a tray . . .' (p. 53), and moves to recall old Mr Earnshaw coming in and calling her 'a cant lass', and from that 'to think of his fondness for Heathcliff, and his dread lest he should suffer neglect' (p. 54).

But we note that these halcyon moments of meditation tend to speak with the narrative voice and to stand abstracted from the action itself. The velocity of the novel is provided by the state of communal and violent tantrum which is indulged not only by the characters against one another but also reverberates outward against the walls of the universe, threatening the gods. Invective against the state of things in this nether world takes the form of a feud with the Maker, exemplified by Hindley's riposte to Nelly's injunction to '"Have mercy on your own soul!"': '"Not I! on the contrary, I shall have great pleasure in sending it to perdition, to punish its maker"', drinking meanwhile to his own damnation and uttering 'horrid imprecations' (p. 75). Clearly, the origins of this profane verbal behaviour lie in the dissatisfactions common to childhood with the provisions and principles laid down by the elders. Hindley's brag has its roots in the juvenile desire evinced in some such formulation as 'I'll make my parents sorry they ever had me'. *Wuthering Heights* systematically translates this vernacular into the language of religious experience, attaching the interior situation of siblings struggling in a domestic world to a higher register of diction which raises them to the elemental status of souls exclaiming against their God. Translation from one discourse into another also, inevitably, involves subtle shifts within the meanings of the original material. Attitudes and moods which within the family context may (from the outside) appear immature take on through literary transference an heroic and magnetic fascination and capability of universal human application, since of course at the very centre of Christian mythology is a cosmic story of disobedient children in mutiny against the divine Parent: Lucifer and Eve. It is here that the authorial mythologising of the ferocious raw material of childhood utterance derives from the latter a genuinely religious vision which carries for the reader the 'higher' meanings and implications of *Wuthering Heights*. From this perspective, the novel becomes a sardonic, wilful and travestying—but perfectly logical and coherent—variation on the Calvinism with which Emily and her siblings were force-fed in childhood;[16] a vision of a reprobated universe in which God's brood, doomed from the start, chooses demonically with Him against its own election and salvation. The first Catherine is the major voice for this heresy: '"heaven did not seem to be my home"' (p. 80), '"they may bury me twelve feet deep, and throw the church down over me"' (p. 126), with Heathcliff playing Beelzebub to her Lucifer. It is focused within speeches and carried by the narrative line during certain phases of the action (see p. 128–45 below) in a joint proclamation of what amounts to extreme Protestant defiance. The novel nails its *Theses* to the church door with relish and acrimony.

At the same time, it locates an alternative area of the divine to that of the Father–God. Deep in its own experience of lack, absence and loss, the psyche in *Wuthering Heights* perceives a spiritual home identifiable with the mother. A void in the communal life of the characters (the first generation of mothers, Catherine and Frances, die in or just after childbirth) is wistfully transferred, and thence to some degree filled, to a new location in the created and suffering universe itself. Beneath the action of the novel, readers are impressed by their intuition of the attending and waiting presence of the moor, despite the seldom-noted fact that it is barely described in physical terms during the crucial first half of the novel. It receives, endorses and forgives; or rather, endorses the fact that there is nothing to forgive. It is the realm of silence and retreat, a playground for children; the mythic ground of action. Beyond the human focus of desire (Catherine's love for Heathcliff) is implied the larger object of desire (Catherine's love for the heath). On the psychological level, the children's refusal of control in *Wuthering Heights* is also a mute demand for the embrace that gathers the child in to himself, providing the limit to his ire and destructiveness. The voices exhibit the combined relish and terror of the uncontrolled idiom that distorts the face of childhood into that of a monster, magnifying its angers into a demonic threat to existence itself. The means of such embrace (the mother) is almost wholly absent from the text, though its children rage and wail loudly enough to wake the dead. Nelly, rocking on her knee the motherless Hareton, hums a snatch of a ballad from Scott: 'It was far in the night, and the bairnies grat,/The mither beneath the mools heard that' (p. 76). In the song, as I have shown elsewhere,[17] the natural mother awakens in her grave at the keening of her orphaned children tortured by their stepmother. Her corpse trespasses across the barrier of mortality, impelled by the fiat of their grief, to remedy their situation. The motherless author of *Wuthering Heights* releases the voices of her characters as a universal cry of need. The novel records both the potency of that need and its absolute failure to register or to obtain the satisfaction of a reply. Yet each time we reread, this fearful hope is freshly aroused, and the novel with profound artfulness never denies that either the dead may walk with us or we sleep with them, in the fullest reunion.

The familial world is controlled at best by a foster-mother (Nelly) together with a kind father (the elder Mr Earnshaw, Edgar Linton), at worst by 'Devil Daddy' (Hindley, Heathcliff). Nelly's prose style, with its curious nullity and blankness of emotional response, neutralises and frustrates the hysterical compulsions recorded in direct speech. Hence the novel's language of desire is constantly being absorbed into a thick, muffling wall of incomprehension:

She paused, and hid her face in the folds of my gown; but I

jerked it forcibly away. I was out of patience with her folly! (p. 82)

She rung the bell till it broke with a twang: I entered leisurely. It was enough to try the temper of a saint, such senseless, wicked rages! (p. 118)

He began to pace the room, muttering terrible things to himself; till I was inclined to believe, as he said Joseph did, that conscience had turned his heart to an earthly hell—I wondered greatly how it would end. (p. 325)

As narrator, Nelly's cool management of domestic affairs on the page is ambivalent, distanced and unwittingly implicated. Narrative and direct speech are frequently at odds. The aim of the censorious, censoring narrative is to mute and suppress the raw emotions indulged by the direct speech; to obscure its meaning as consciousness seals the unconscious into inscrutability. In the second half of the novel, the language of desire is displaced by a general rise in the 'dream-material' toward consciousness and synthesis with the narrative voice: a transformation of prehistory into history, or dream-matter into conscious thought, as if a sleeper gradually awakened. The exception to this rule is Heathcliff, in whose accounts of his state of mind to Nelly the original language of desire endures but tends to shift into a brilliant and scintillating language of marvellous dissatisfaction such as characterises much of Emily Brontë's lyric poetry. Heathcliff's ' "My soul's bliss kills my body, but does not satisfy itself" ' (p. 333), for instance, recalls the visionary prisoner of 'Julian M. and A.G. Rochelle': 'visions rise and change which kill me with desire' (l. 72). Death as a release from this galled and excoriated nervous condition is apprehended by the novel as rest and succour in a mother-world which resolves the conflicts of the upper world in a completion born not of settling scores by bargain or forgiveness, nor of reaching adjustment with things as they are (that is, by growing up), but by entering into the being of the beloved, in shared sleep. Heathcliff's 'transformation' (p. 289) into the substance of Catherine underground, to which he looks forward with famishing eagerness, is the falling asleep of a lifelong insomniac, entering into the balm of the subliminal world, which gives entire permission to his every desire by abolishing in its entirety the wordy, needy self. Language and desire cease simultaneously; the heath, clambering over the low church wall on to the threefold graves of Catherine, Edgar Linton and Heathcliff, is finally observed to be occupied in the process of erasing the writing which signs their presence to the upper world: the names on the headstones. Burying their individualities in itself, the moor takes its children home.

Chapter Two

The Dictates of Civility

Emily Brontë's religion of childhood consecrates it as a period of devastating sublimity, without denying its utter vulnerability to pain. It equates it with perfect freedom, whilst acknowledging its constriction by despotic parental law. It praises the life of absolutes, the refusal of compromise or qualification either to love or hate, though it knows the dangerous impracticality of such life. Most strenuously, it celebrates a kind of preposterous honesty and directness of speech and action which characterise that early world, and which, when liberated on to the field of adult experience, renovate and revolutionise the entire social perspective. This is especially true in relation to gender. Gender-roles are consummately without meaning to the children of the novel: hence there is an overwhelming experience of unfallen freedom (for the boy in the girl, the girl in the boy—the sharing of identity between Catherine and Heathcliff): '"he's more myself than I am. Whatever our souls are made of, his and mine are the same"' (p80); '"he's always, always in my mind...as my own being"' (p.82); '"I wish I were a girl again, half savage and hardy, and free"' (p.126); '"Oh, Cathy! Oh, my life"' (p.158); '"she was...resting her darling head on the same pillow as she did when a child"' (p.290). These examples belong to a pattern of strong-willed utterance dedicated to disruption of the common parlance of gender-specialisation upon which civilised life is hierarchically constructed. Its synthesis of opposites is as intolerable to the social order as the transgression of any taboo which is held to ensure norms of behaviour. A girlhood 'savage and hardy, *and free*' (emphasis added) which projects itself upon the figure of a ruffianly male companion, challenges the language of caste (based on analysis of difference) by synthesising male and female to androgynous 'soul' or 'life': the Jungian *animus* and *anima*.[1]

This is, of course, far more true of the first generation of the novel's children, for the second—Catherine II, Linton Heathcliff, Hareton—are raised as only children, split off from the original group, and have to work their way back to a version of this familial union. The second Catherine's query, '"what are those golden rocks...? I can go, too, when I am a woman"' (p.189), signals her innate intuition of being reared in a state of dislocation from one pole of her affinity. But the second generation represents a displacement, dilution and (except for the *lusus naturae*, Linton Heathcliff, who as a kind of albino has to be bred out) a regularisation of the original characters. Even so, there is never a standardisation toward the conventional social norm of the child's-eye-view with which Emily Brontë re-creates the social world. In the second and recapitulating half of the novel, the reader is preoccupied with linked acts of remembrance as the second story shadows the first with significant variations, the second Catherine calls back to the first with each telling of her name on the page, and Heathcliff like a living ghost frequently passing before our eyes testifies to the present tense as a mere aftermath to reality.

The ethos of *Wuthering Heights* never yields to the dictates of civility. So cunningly, however, does the author imply a norm of mores, etiquette and decorous behaviour (through the stratified class world, the narrators' approving or adverse comment, and the unquestioned mechanisms of domestic life—laying fires, taking tea, attending to livestock) that few readers register the fact that Emily Brontë's perspective omits certain normal social pressures and expectations from her novel. It is a crucial and revolutionary avoidance. We may trace and evaluate this oblique deviation from the imperatives of social form through small but telling details of usage, particularly within the Linton household, which functions as a norm against which we are invited to judge the bad behaviour of the Earnshaw establishment. In the supposedly 'adult' world of Thrushcross Grange, Edgar Linton responds to the liaison between Catherine and Heathcliff in the following terms:

> "To get rid of me—answer my question," persevered Mr. Linton. "You *must* answer it; and that violence does not alarm me. I have found that you can be as stoical as any one, when you please. Will you give up Heathcliff hereafter, or will you give up me? It is impossible for you to be *my* friend and *his* at the same time; and I absolutely *require* to know which you choose."
>
> (p. 118)

In the world of childhood, one recalls, the most smartingly abusive terms of threat are founded in the withdrawal of allegiance: 'I shan't be your friend *any more!*' Such a threat is rooted in a language implicitly egalitarian, democratic and not gender-specific. The politics of the adult and 'civilised' world rest on a power-structure hierarchically designed, and loaded against the female with a most killing weight of property-based, mandated power-terminology. 'I am your *husband*', Edgar might have reminded Catherine, 'and *he* may not be your "friend" any more'. From this basis in legal privilege the imperative 'I absolutely *require*' would have accrued the authority which in Emily Brontë's theatre it so splendidly lacks. Hence the author communicates to the world of her novel (and, we would guess, to the pre-existing world of Gondal) a quality of freedom, even within the orphanage-world's privations and rivalries, for which the adult world as we know it offers no exact correlative. Emily Brontë never subjects Catherine to the institutionalised pressures of male society such as those to which George Eliot subjects Dorothea Casaubon, condemning her to 'bear this nightmare of a life in which every energy was arrested by dread' (*Middlemarch*, Ch. 37, p. 410), and Gwendolen Grandcourt's subjection to 'her husband's empire of fear' (*Daniel Deronda*, Ch. 35, p. 479).[2] To make this comparison is to highlight the extent to which the youthfulness of Emily Brontë's novel liberates the world of the two Catherines from the tyranny of the world of the fathers, in which George Eliot's epic narrator and epic heroines are engrossed. It is as if Emily Brontë had pursued—in the secluded north, largely self-educated, guarded from the confusions and perplexities of young ladies' education, free of the enfeebling and taming influence of a natural mother—a course of separate development. The stigma, cross and moral incentive of Victorian womanhood was a sense of guilt.[3] Society inscribed through reinforcement of guilt feelings a punitive and self-hurting code of behaviour upon the inmost tissue of the individual self: guilt atrophied initiative and muted utterance, at source. The work of Emily Brontë displays a unique immunity to such guilt. She had rejected point-blank the weight of her female inheritance; had refused to come of age in order to elude it.

Emily Brontë was 27 when she wrote *Wuthering Heights*; George Eliot, born only a year later than Emily, was just over 50 at the time of writing *Middlemarch*, and in her late fifties when she composed *Daniel Deronda*. George Eliot's heroines have internalised the pressures of the society into which they are born; Emily Brontë's Catherine displays a fanatical resistance to such pressures as are brought to bear on her. She feels 'split', it is true, and ultimately dies for it: but it is a clean break. She undergoes no such 'uneasy, transforming process' as undermines Gwendolen, sifting through to the root of her being like a chemical transformation. George Eliot discloses the implications of living within the medium of a world of which one's aspirations furnish such a small, fragile and impotent part: she divulges half a century of such experience on to the page, a cosmopolitan and universal experience for woman of her tragic susceptibility to mastery which reaches through and through her being. Emily Brontë exhibits Catherine's difference from the society which seeks to contain her spirits, as a species of glorious maladjustment. George Eliot strives for a difficult process of integration in heroines distinctly comparable with Catherine. The pain of integration, with accompanying recognition of the network of complexity in which all men and women are bound, the urge toward intellectual and moral clarification, a benign work in life and articulation of such clear perception as is attained, motivate the plot, character and ethos within her novels.[4] Such incorporation of the moral world by the adaptive ego, with reciprocal assimilation of character into the world, is foreign to the experience of Emily Brontë's novel. Charlotte was sure—or declared herself sure—that if Emily had survived her youth, she would have adapted to the world in the manner of a tree maturing:

> Had she but lived, her mind would of itself have grown like a strong tree, loftier, straighter, wider-spreading, and its matured fruits would have attained a mellower ripeness and summer bloom; but on that mind time and experience alone could work: to the influence of other itellects, it was not amenable.
>
> ('Editor's Preface to the New Edition of *Wuthering Heights*',
> p. 367)

'Wider-spreading': Charlotte indicates a desirable comprehensiveness of vision, extending the self in sympathy and understanding. The first half of the sentence sounds as if Charlotte were envisaging, in the orchard of her metaphor, the burgeoning of a more cultivable mentality in her sister than is discernible in *Wuthering Heights*. Emily's remote narrowness would, she feels, temper and relax with age: but the second half of the sentence is humanly chilling in its recognition that Emily Brontë was and would remain inflexibly maladaptive. Constitutionally resistant to 'the influence of other intellects', Emily Brontë was the artist of the intransigently singular self. Charlotte Brontë seems to have felt—or, more probably, vaguely wished—that somehow, she could have 'ripened', grown up, whilst refusing the imprint of influence, through 'time' and 'experience' alone. Time to do what? Charlotte does not say. Emily Brontë would certainly have been rooted to the spot, refusing the proximity of her kind, tuned to the authority of her earliest source: 'those first feelings that were born in me', 'the love that first its glory gave'.[5]

She is, in this sense of refusing to join the human community the radical opposite of George Eliot. Because she kept so closely to the sources of energy in the androgynous dynamic of childhood, she licenses Catherine's vivacity where George Eliot must chasten that of her heroines.[6] Neither Catherine Earnshaw nor Gwendolen Harleth is a corrigible entity: each has a flaunting, vagrant tongue, an imaginative and nervous disposition, a moral awareness so flimsy as to be negligible. But Catherine *Linton* is permitted to remain recognisably Catherine Earnshaw—under pressure, in conflict: Gwendolen *Grandcourt* must not so much part company with Gwendolen Harleth as undergo transformation, slow, painful, minute, through every particle of her being. She is not her own; is Grandcourt's property, under the terms of the marriage licence (Blackstone's famous formulation: 'Man and wife are one person under the law, and that person is the husband').[7] In another sense, she is her creator's subjected and deflated victim, dragged through the mesh of chemical change, so that she can never again be her first self. Even to cut off the existence of her husband, as Gwendolen seeks to do, is not to achieve the liberation of a return; on the contrary, she is stranded with the consciousness of her own inchoate 'small life' (Ch. 69, p. 876) in the vast crucible of the moral world. All narrative energies tend to this point: that for woman, susceptible biologically, legally and psychologically, as she is, there is no backtracking to the dream-time when she called her soul her own, had a 'sense of superior claims' (Ch. 2, p. 44) and 'felt ready to manage her own destiny' (Ch. 4, p. 70). We see her falter and fall; hear her voice become shaken and tremulous. Emily Brontë authorises an opposite journey: the way home is always potentially open. 'Often rebuked, but always back returning', the homing soul is free to try the far-fetched journey across open countryside to redeem its beginnings. *Wuthering Heights* is a myth of freedom. Catherine Linton never leaves off being Catherine Earnshaw. Like the caged bird of Emily's poem, the 'prisoned soul'[8] frets against its bars to obtain a final release. The visions of Emily Brontë and George Eliot are logically incompatible. Whereas childhood is the source of power and a kind of amoral beauty in *Wuthering Heights* even when a version of it is perpetuated into adult life, in George Eliot it can be a source of liability or a kind of fatal softness: Maggie Tulliver's yearning allegiances, Dorothea's 'childlike' emotional susceptibility and naïveté, her aptness to 'sob' her words out on grand occasions.[9] But in Emily Brontë, the child's—and adult child's—cries of joy and pain are paeons of vivacity, displays of aerobatic temperament which carry their own heady language glorying in its own eccentricity. The licence Emily Brontë preserves in the world of her art is clear if we compare the conditions assigned by the author to Catherine's marriage:

> I got Miss Catherine and myself to Thrushcross Grange: and to my agreeable disappointment, she behaved infinitely better than I dared to expect. She seemed almost over fond of Mr. Linton; and even to his sister, she showed plenty of affection. They were both very attentive to her comfort, certainly. It was not the thorn bending to the honeysuckles, but the honeysuckles embracing the thorn. There were no mutual concessions; one stood erect, and the others yielded; and who *can* be ill-natured and bad-tempered, when they encounter neither opposition nor indifference?
>
> I observed that Mr. Edgar had a deep-rooted fear of ruffling her humour. He concealed it from her; but if ever

he heard me answer sharply, or saw any other servant grow
cloudy at some imperious order of hers, he would show his
trouble by a frown of displeasure that never darkened on
his own account.   (p. 91)

with those assigned to Gwendolen Harleth:

This beautiful, healthy young creature, with her two-and-
twenty years and her gratified ambition, no longer felt
inclined to kiss her fortunate image in the glass; she looked
at it with wonder that she could be so miserable. One belief
which had accompanied her through her unmarried life as a
self-cajoling superstition, encouraged by the subordination
of every one about her—the belief in her own power of
dominating—was utterly gone. Already, in seven short
weeks, which seemed half her life, her husband had gained
a mastery which she could no more resist than she could
have resisted the benumbing effect from the touch of a
torpedo. Gwendolen's will had seemed imperious in its
small girlish sway; but it was the will of a creature with a
large discourse of imaginative fears: a shadow would have
been enough to relax its hold.
                          (*Daniel Deronda*, Ch. 35, p. 477)

The narrative voice in the *Wuthering Heights* passage is
sulkily disapproving of Linton's uxoriousness and
Catherine's unexpected compliance in her new state, but
we are given to understand the motivation of Nelly's
attitude, and do not necessarily concur. Emily Brontë
enacts her customary 'sinistral' reversal of that traditional and Miltonic imagery which insinuates a justification in the natural order for the politics of gender by
identifying the sexes with species displaying innately
'dependent' or 'independent' characteristics. Catherine's
inflexibility and dominance, figured in the thorn which
will not bend to the honeysuckle, with its predatory and
derivative life, swoops down on the Miltonic paradigm in

Paradise Lost, Book IV, and reverses its terms, to saturnalian effect. Eve's hair:

> in wanton ringlets waved
> As the vine curls her tendrils, which implied
> Subjection, but required with gentle sway
>
> (IV.306–8)

In traditional iconography, the 'male' prop supports the 'female' vine; the 'female' woodbine clasps the honeysuckle; the 'male' elm maintains the 'female' ivy.[10] Emily Brontë's heroine is not a deviant parasite asserting an incredible autonomy but a free-standing 'thorn' (bred of the wilderness and adapted to life outside Eden) which *cannot* if it tries defy its own nature to obey the dictates of civility. Catherine and Edgar are differentiated as species rather than by gender. The Miltonic condition of man's 'erect' stature, woman's 'yielding' posture (*PL* IV.289–311) reverses neatly ('one stood erect, and the others yielded') as the two Lintons, both gendered 'feminine' in terms of the novel's structuring polarities of innate characteristics, concede to the despotism of the rough-hewn Earnshaw temperament. Edgar protects himself against his own fear of Catherine by rebuking Nelly for crossing her. The 'deep and growing happiness' which Nelly thinks she detects in the couple (p. 92) is hence patently—to the reader—frail, flawed and delicate.

Everything in the narrative stresses the superficiality of the hold Edgar has on Catherine, and his own uneasy sense of insecurity in relation to her ascendency. It is only his fear which is termed 'deep-rooted'; he lives under a virtual gynarchy, by recourse to a system of concealments and secondary manoeuvrings, signalling to third parties whom he *can* control (the servants) to make space for a nature which he has no means to command. His defensive manipulations are the traditional 'women's weapons' for preserving the peace. It is Catherine's incorruptible freedom which he fears; her self-elected licence to assert her self. The author deprives Linton of access to the legal and psychological machinery of suppression which (as Anne Brontë ruthlessly illustrates in *The Tenant of Wildfell Hall*) was freely available to any nineteenth-century husband. The disarmed male in Emily Brontë's vision—disempowered by his worshipping tenderness for his wife, as well as by his incapacity to possess her—permits a radical rephrasing of the possibilities for man as he might be if he remained more fully his mother's child into adult life than society considers desirable. The novel reinforces this vision of Edgar as a 'mother's son' through the imagery it casts upon him—intended as opprobrium by the unruly speakers, but open to kinder interpretation by the reader. Edgar is, according to Heathcliff's insolence, '"this lamb of yours"' (p. 114), '"not a lamb... a sucking leveret"' (Catherine, p. 115), '"milk-blooded coward"' (Heathcliff, p. 115). The milk that flows in Edgar's veins creates the impression not of weakness (that deviation from the Linton authenticity we view in his spiteful and craven namesake, Linton Heathcliff) but a species of aberrant strength, the focus of the novel's considerable leaven of gentleness, strikingly memorable for his explicitly maternal and nurturing care of Catherine in her last illness (p. 134).[11]

Turning from the *Wuthering Heights* to the *Daniel Deronda* extract, we register the full impact of the crushing force George Eliot brings down upon her heroine's original life-energies, to which the contract of her marriage—and, to a degree, the subtly concurrent judgement of the narrator—has subjected her. Marriages undertaken in the course of Eliot's novels—

Romola's with Tito, Dorothea's with Casaubon, Gwendolen's with Grandcourt—tend to function for the young woman as irrevocable initiations from the narcissistic world of 'girlish sway' when, like Gwendolen, she 'felt inclined to kiss her fortunate image in the glass' across the threshold into the punitive light of day. Marriage brings full revelation of woman's disempowered position in so far as her autonomy is concerned: George Eliot's narrative systematically strips Gwendolen of access to the terminology of power and choice: *subordination, power of dominating, mastery, resist, imperious.* All such terms are conceded to the husband. The narrative holds Gwendolen in a vice: requiring that she shall change and adapt to the realities of the world in which her desire forms so insignificant a part. *Daniel Deronda* is a scourging of vanity in which the vulnerable, lacerated ego resists its cure until the bitter end. Gwendolen's late moment of grace comes when she 'submitted like a half-soothed child', sobbing out to Daniel, '"I said... I said... it should be better... better with me... for having known you"' (Ch. 69, p. 878). The small-voiced, chastened language of concession belongs to George Eliot's Nonconformist heritage: the language of contrition—all pauses and echoes—the ardent voice of self-subdued to a ghost of its originality.[12]

To make the George Eliot/Emily Brontë comparison is to broach the polar oppositions within female creativity, the one dedicated to the ethical as prior and primary (if ambiguous and difficult), the other steadfastly declaring aversion to the dictates of civility. The passage from Emily Brontë's account of the union of Catherine and Edgar concludes in an icy-cool repudiation of the long-term practicality of a life consciously addressing itself to the Good, against the bias of inclination:

It ended. Well, we *must* be for ourselves in the long run; the mild and generous are only more justly selfish than the domineering—and it ended when circumstances caused each to feel that the one's interest was not the chief consideration in the other's thoughts.

On a mellow evening in September, I was coming from the garden with a heavy basket of apples which I had been gathering. It had got dusk, and the moon looked over the high wall of the court (p. 92)

It ended: the ruthlessly conclusive narrative voice records what it perceives as an inevitable outcome, given the universal raw material which constitutes human nature. It declares and then not only rationalises but justifies the limited tenure of the Linton marriage. The narrative *we* implicates narrator and outer narrator (Lockwood), protagonists and the reader in its utilitarian felicific calculus. The author herself remains, of course, uncommitted, and no authoritative status is attached to Nelly's ego-centred philosophy of life; we may (as ever) assent or dissent, the text is frankly indifferent. But plot, character, and dialogue, both in detail and as a totality, verify the insight. The primacy of self—its irrepressible endurance beneath the surface of received behaviour, in its full potency—is demonstrated by the plot's declaration of Heathcliff at this transitional moment. Heathcliff's return, to violate the 'deep and growing happiness' imputed to the married couple, figures a powerful resurgence of Catherine's own dormant self. He thrusts his path back into the picture with a quality of omen, like a messenger from another (and threatening) world, or like the contents of the buried seed piercing the ground, with the ferocity of a force of nature.

The narrative voice yields to this intrusion with a sudden break into pastoral: its tone modulates into a wistful evocation of 'a mellow evening in September'. Nelly is like the apple-woman, Pomona with her basket,

Eve the gatherer of ripe mortality. The air is clement and heavy with collected fragrances, the evening's beauty appearing numinous with shadows, and within these shadows the implied expectations of presences. Nelly pauses to study the moon, and it is in this aura of musing quietness that the intrusive voice is heard ('deep ... and foreign in tone ... familiar'). This mood, and the configuration of imagery inscribed upon it—a 'mellow'[13] moonlit or starlit evening, an intrusive 'wanderer' or 'messenger' whose appearance is associated simultaneously with the quickening of Eros and the proximity of Death—is a Byronic motif in Emily Brontë's poetry recurrently associated with the quickening of the creative sensibility. Heathcliff's very existence is an affront to good manners; he is the illicit access forged (at the price of life itself) from the subconscious to the conscious world. His lack of a past exempts him from Time but commits him to origins; he is Catherine before she fell into her adult female biology and status. He represents her self indefinitely extended into androgynous liberty within the mother-world. Yet Heathcliff is resurrected as the demon-lover of the ballad dressed for a funeral 'in dark clothes, with dark face and hair' (p. 92), both a primordial and a mortal figure, spelling disruption and death to the indoor world for which Nelly acts as Janus, the ambiguous doorkeeper and mediator. His welcome into the narrative, however, is entranced and lyrical; his emergence signalled by the grace of a prose which seems to carry an otherworldly and transcendent dream-aura: the reposeful girl burdened with apples, the moon, the balmy night-airs. At this moment the entrance to the underworld is gaping wide open; Heathcliff is declared to the upper world as the electrifying and spellbinding hoardings of the imagination.

Readers have long been struck by the curious aura of

sexual purity which invests the passionate physical responses made by the central characters to one another. In 1850 Sydney Dobell noted 'the involuntary art with which [Catherine's] two natures are so made to co-exist, that in the very arms of her lover we dare not doubt her purity'.[14] One effect of *Wuthering Heights* may be to reproduce a state of mind in the reader which impersonates the pre-moral,[15] prior to the assimilation of those social sanctions which determine in us a language of guilt. The very diction and grammar of *Wuthering Heights*, and especially its subtle absence of inflection, have the effect of seeming to retract the consciousness to a point before we fell into the full-scale, life-consuming enterprise of praising and blaming. The patterns of the novel's language imply a retreat into the archaic, eschewing a language of consensus taboo which may be essential to the stability of sociable life in a community. If such patterns are wished on us by our participation in the narrative voice and reproduced in us by our silent recital of words of prelapsarian (i.e. uncensored) desire, as we read, then it may be possible to see the experience of reading *Wuthering Heights* as a submission to demoralisation, in which we are systematically stripped of Christian and civilised values. *Wuthering Heights* as an act of reading becomes the innocent eating of the forbidden fruit.

Certainly, this novel is a mouthpiece for need: need vast, uncouth, disfiguring and ravenous. It speaks not for individuals nor on behalf of one caste, race, age-group or gender, but—as Virginia Woolf intuited—seeks 'to say something through the mouths of her characters which is not merely "I love you" or "I hate", but "we, the whole human race" and "you, the eternal powers..." The sentence remains unfinished.'[16] Hence, Emily Brontë, like George Eliot[17] but more elementally, through the double narrator (male and female tellers, Lockwood-

Nelly) mediating two sets of double male-and-female heroes (Catherine–Heathcliff, Catherine–Hareton) enacts an expression of transcendently human rather than partial and feminine truth. *Wuthering Heights'* universality derives to a considerable degree from this multiple identification of *anima* with *animus*. It declares itself in the infinite-seeming ramifications of the one plight, the mirroring-out of a plurality of patterns and distortions of pattern in a cosmos which structures the reverberations of the story's central narcissism within tight concentricities of narrative form. In turn, this narrative structure is a dynamic binding-together of the polarities of human experience: a containment for the story which, like Catherine's panelled bed, figures both womb and tomb. Heathcliff is central to this universal cry of need, a focus and activation of suffering: a turbulent voice of desire which, in the end (like Echo, the survivor of Narcissus) is *nothing but* the voice of want. Heathcliff is an act of utterance on the part of the author for Love as lack. With Catherine's death he becomes void, absence, a gap demanding to be filled, a mouth for feeding. 'Love is in love with what he lacks and does not possess', says Plato's Socrates' Diotima in the *Symposium,* in a structure as devious and subversive.[18]

But the need which *Wuthering Heights* articulates goes beyond even the extreme case of human hardship. It is a novel which uniquely speaks of and for the suffering of the whole orphaned Creation, as one with the need experienced by God's vocally human children. The access it allows to the energies of the unconscious mind relates to its parallel identification with the intuitive world of creatures in a carnivorous nature. Catherine's 'lapwing' speech is a powerful and profound instance of the novel's reaching out beyond the frontier of the

human community toward parity with a full range of
creaturely existence:

> 'and this—I should know it among a thousand—it's a
> lapwing's. Bonny bird; wheeling over our heads in the
> middle of the moor. It wanted to get to its nest, for the
> clouds touched the swells, and it felt rain coming. This
> feather was picked up from the heath, the bird was not
> shot—we saw its nest in the winter, full of little skeletons.
> Heathcliff set a trap over it, and the old ones dare not come.
> I made him promise he'd never shoot a lapwing, after that,
> and he didn't. Yes, here are more! Did he shoot my
> lapwings, Nelly? Are they red, any of them? Let me look.'
>
> (pp. 122–3)

The 'nest in the winter, full of little skeletons' is
important both as a visual reflection of the human
subject of the novel, and as an additional subject in itself.
As metaphor, it displays the emotional condition of the
novel's children; the trap set over the nest to interfere
with the communion of 'the old ones' with their young
may be read as an elegy on Mr Earnshaw dead, Edgar
Linton dying, mother-loss, God recorded across the
whole scope of the novel as an absentee. But in recording
the absence, cruelty or impotence of the Creator, the
animal world forsakes its role as analogy on the periphery
of the fictional world to focus a universal condition of
which Catherine herself is only an instance. In her
wanderings, she extends her love to the lapwing—
'Bonny bird...'—in a gesture of affinity and celebration.
These are 'my lapwings', elected, adopted into her benign
protection, as being connected for her with the mythic
centre of the centre, 'the middle of the moor'. In her
dream, we recollect, the angels had flung her from
heaven '"into the middle of the heath on the top of
Wuthering Heights; where I woke sobbing for joy"' (p.

80): the centric sanctuary of permitted desire, the paradise she greedily falls into. Catherine's imagery describes the effect of complete encirclement: the 'wheeling' bird; the raised faces of the children; the 'swells' with their breastlike contour, the circular nest. But Catherine's narrative vitiates the symbolic circle of divinely panoramic protection and eternity, suiting the image of devastation to the harsh and bloody pastoral in which *Wuthering Heights* is rooted. The parent-bird circles in panic for home; the sky has fallen on the swells; the nest will expose the underlying rhyme of *womb* and *tomb*. Heathcliff (the lawless cuckoo in the human nest) mediates the two worlds of human and animal: the speech registers him as an inhuman presence in the natural world, a predator whose restraint even she cannot feel sure of guaranteeing: '"Did he shoot my lapwings, Nelly?"' Heathcliff's motiveless ferocity in making a sacrificial slaughter of the innocents imitates— or personifies—a principle in nature, just as his cries of fear and loss articulate the pains of that same mute creation. The orphaned destroyer takes his place on the Chain of Being as a fellow participant in an inclusive struggle for survival which is the inheritance of all sentient life.

At Law Hill, Emily Brontë had told the recalcitrant school-children that the only creature she could take to on the premises was the house-dog.[19] *Wuthering Heights* testifies to an analogous preference. This misanthropist's heaven is the habitation of families of dogs, named and pedigreed with authorial care, and imparting a quality of insanely comic vivacity to the interior domestic world penetrated by Lockwood's clueless eye. For instance, 'the canine mother's' slavering assault on the intrusive narrator ('sneaking wolfishly to the back of my legs, her lip curled up, and her white teeth watering for a snatch' [p. 4])—interpreted by Lockwood's choicely and anarchically metaphor-breeding mind into samples of the Gadarene swine (p. 5) or a 'brood of tigers'—is a potent sentinel to the subliminal meanings housed at the Heights. These meanings belong to human nature seen *in a continuum* with animal nature. It was said that affection for animals was a touchstone for acceptability with Emily Brontë for visitors to the Parsonage.[20] By these standards Lockwood disqualifies himself from serious consideration by a range of early activities: mistaking 'a heap of dead rabbits' for Cathy's 'favourites', pet kittens; pulling faces at Heathcliff's three dogs. Through Lockwood's discomfiture we see the gender-specific, caste bound social world of human marriage, its estate, customs and the priority of its linguistic usages as determining the novelist's conventions and usages systematically ridiculed and tossed aside: the wife as '"amiable lady...presiding genius over...home and heart"' (p. 11), '"beneficent fairy"' (p. 12). The novel will concern itself with mating rather than with marriage; with the human household in its proximity to the wilderness of the moorland, home both of predator and prey, twinned victims whose intimate alliance is mirrored in the instinctual life of the human protagonists.

Emily Brontë's conception of Mother Nature appears to underlie the entire action; but Emily Brontë has moved from a Wordsworthian trust in the maternal tenderness of the natural world to a pre-Darwinian evolutionary theology of nature, as a universal power-struggle in which all creatures and Creation itself are forced to contend.[21] Hence the feuding world of her characters reproduces the state of nature in domestic relations: the Earnshaw/Linton/Heathcliff turbulence impresses us as a fragment of a cosmic pain, visited upon the natural world by the external agency of a senseless God. The statement of some such heresy may be read in her 1842 devoir, entitled *Le Papillon:*

> la création entière est également insensée. Voilà, ces mouches jouant au dessus du ruisseau, des hirondelles et des poissons en diminuent le nombre chaque minute: ceux-ci deviendront, en leur tour, la proie de quelque tyron de l'air ou de l'eau: et l'homme pour son amusement ou pour ses besoins, tuera leurs meurtiers. La nature est un problème inexplicable, elle existe sur un principe de destruction; il faut que tout être soit l'instrument infatigable de mort aux autres, ou qu'il cesse de vivre lui-même;...en ce moment l'univers me paraissait une vaste machine construite seulement pour produire la mal.
>
> (Gérin, pp. 271–2)

In another essay, *Le Chat,* the 24 year old Emily commented on the bloodily comparable spectacles of an angelic and kissable child whose hand opens to disclose a butterfly broken by his sadistic little fingers, and a cat trailing the tail of half-eaten prey from his mouth. We may remember Edgar Linton who 'possessed the power to depart [from Catherine], as much as a cat possesses the power to leave a mouse half killed, or a bird half eaten' (p. 72), or Catherine warning Isabella, '"he's a fierce, pitiless, wolfish man...he'd crush you, like a sparrow's egg"' (p. 102). Domestication and civilisation are not even skin-deep, in these images of dispassionate natural cruelty. Petted human child and pet cat are the products of the one agency, 'un principe de destruction', the senseless blood-drive on which the whole famishing, bewildered creation is predicated. *Le Papillon* artfully presents this perception as a saturnine mood only, and claims to contradict it with an explication of the life-cycle of the butterfly as a legend of transformation in whose terms 'ce globe est l'embrion d'un nouveau ciel et d'une nouvelle terre' (p. 272). However, the legend of Psyche which I think hovers behind *Wuthering Heights*[22] is not at odds with Emily Brontë's vision of the creation as a great abattoir-world in which all are implicated and all are absolved of blame: the implied myth offers succour within the terms of that vision. As Psyche seeks her self in Cupid, Catherine and Heathcliff seek amorous fusion of unconscious self with self beneath the surface of the blood-stained earth. The resolution of conflict in the *quiet earth* (see pp. 146–55 below) is also entrance to that 'other world' of Catherine's yearning. The deathward tendency of Emily Brontë's imaginative journey seems to have been felt as curative and consolatory in so far as it ordained a pilgrimage toward union with the *insentient* basis and matrix of mother nature—a vegetative as opposed to an animal state of being—heath and harebells, grasses and trees, which presented to her becalmed senses a principle of decisive and energetic life exempted from the tainting inheritance of mortal pain. The large spaces of the moors, seen in this light, become a visionary resting-ground for the past which is also a growing-place for the quick, emergent life of every shoot and blade on which the eye may glut itself. The underworld declares itself, a gospel, in messages of green:

> Only some spires of bright green grass
> Transparently in sunlight quivering

This imagist fragment may stand for the whole corpus of her poetry as the epitome of its celebration of the rapturously free insentience of the rooted world. The child's-eye-view was required to decode these messages. Interpreted thus, the archetype *Mother Nature* becomes twofold: the rage of sentient suffering which calls out against its unatoning Creator: the tumultuous peace of insentient growth which may be sought as a sanctuary from the Creator. Hence Emily Brontë's elegies are luminous on the subject of the dark world to be encountered underground, at once holding back from and looking forward to 'The time when my sunny hair/Shall with grass roots twined be' ('In the Earth' ll. 7–8). The weaving of bright human hair with the obscure filaments of roots lends a strange impression of ongoing, purposeful creativity to processes within the buried world: the similitude implies pattern and congruence of activity between the now root-fast human world and the underworld's yielding of life to the vegetation of the upper world.[23] Death as escape into process, 'a new heaven and a new earth', whether in air, earth, water or the body of the beloved, is an escape from exposure to the pain of mother earth to encapsulation in the peace of Mother Earth.

The novel's commitment to a world beyond the human community anticipates Forster's query as to whether Western consciousness (and, by extension, the Western novel) may reasonably hope to embrace all 'humanity grading and drifting beyond the educated vision', and then animal and plant-life, in its promiscuous invitation to all reality to contribute to a totality of meaning.[24] Forster and Emily Brontë recognise this widening of focus in the direction of universality as essentially a religious and iconoclastic exercise. Emily Brontë's enterprise incorporating 'nature' is revolutionary both in terms of the novel, and in terms of the novel as written by a woman. It cancels time-honoured boundaries between social categories—male/female, child/adult—and challenges ancient Western traditions of the Father-God, by presenting a mother-world as the proper end of human desire. In the matrix of this mother-vision, meaning is ruined and remade (just as in the course of *Wuthering Heights* the church is progressively degraded, ruined and restructured into the moorlands). Its oblique, slantwise alignment with the traditional fictive language, narrative authority and the community's ethical-social imperatives, presents an indirect but utterly recalcitrant refusal of submission to patriarchal assumptions of how meaning is generated. In every available literary way, the novel refuses the burden of influence: it announces *Non serviam*. In abolishing the boundaries between genders, in homing in to the core of family as a distillation of significant reality, and adventuring into the always threatening (to art) dimension of nature, Emily Brontë runs risks of creating a working model so congruent with itself and so intolerant of external interpretation, that 'all meaning' is seen as 'no meaning'. 'We must exclude someone from our gathering, or we shall be left with nothing', Forster ironically echoes from the matriarchy of nature in the Marabar whose discouraging riposte to the significant sound-differences encoded as linguistic systems is, indiscriminately, the vacuous 'Boum' (*Passage to India*, pp.38, 145). Emily Brontë's novel does, on the face of it, appear to argue against the accepted meaningful events of human life, being born, growing up, and for the desirability of death. The tenor is sombre. But the tonality of the novel's voices is quite otherwise: it is joyous. Its language, from the wicked ironies of the narrative voice to the dream speech of its lyricism, is pure *jeu d'esprit*. The act of writing appears as the unique means of immortalising and authorising the energies of childhood, whereby words (a sign in themselves of loss, since they occur in a child's development after the initially wordless eye-contact with the mother has been forfeited)[25] are liberated from their original conditions to be inscribed in the form of a homeopathic—not palliative—remedy for the very conditions they record. This action of written language to remedy and redress incurable affliction (not by denying its reality but in direct proportion to the rigour with which the source of pain is divulged and affirmed in its fullness) is essential to the therapy of art. The tonic effect of fictive language may be tested by comparing the different reverberations of an identical language of grief recorded from the 'real' world—in biography—and within the mimetic stylisations of a novel. Thus in the latest biography of Emily Dickinson, the poet is remembered by her niece as repeating over and over again, in response to her father's death, the 'frightening phrase . . . "Where is he? I can't find him".'[26] In *Wuthering Heights*, after Catherine's death, Heathcliff cries out, '"only *do* not leave me in this abyss, where I cannot find you!"' (p. 167; see pp. 58–9 above). The common utterance *I cannot find him/you* reverts in either case to the most primitive of childhood horrors, that of separation from the life-guaranteeing parent, cast in the original dialect of helpless incomprehension. Heathcliff's cry records a loss which may, we assume, have figured in Emily Brontë's life in as personally catastrophic a way as its parallel in Emily Dickinson's. But the act of inscribing the words as a fiction achieves for them the transcendence of heroic gesture. They are savoured for their sublimity and attached to an experience of interpretative vacuum which we can paradoxically locate in a conceptual tradition (the Miltonic 'abyss', associated by Jung[27] with the dark side of the mother archetype). Fictional language here fills the very vacuum it documents. It maps the uncharted territory: a plenitude of energy rushes in to affirm the reality of abeyance. The quoted fragment of Emily Dickinson's speech, on the contrary, even in its written form drains meaning from the language in which it restlessly records its cyclical failure of interpretation of reality. The potency of language to indicate location ('Where...?') is forlornly denied. The words are air. The childlike literality of the idiolect with which she interrogates the visible world for signs of presence persuades us of a loss more abortive than anything fiction can know.

To this degree, the dictates of civility as they are communicated in the resources of fictive language specifically in written language, that most reclusive, subtle and covert act of intimate sharing—were welcomed by Emily Brontë as the means of attaining the equivalent of a state of Grace in a universe born of her own childhood energies and allegiances and composing her legacy of childhood need.

Chapter Three

Brother-and-Sister Love: A Theology of Byronism

Wuthering Heights figures a delinquent but not an illicit love. Man in Emily Brontë retains God in order to appeal to or defy his authority (Joseph on the one hand, Catherine on the other), but he invests in him neither his sense of the holy nor of the lovable. The holy is powerfully there in the novel, but its sanctuary is a forbidden allegiance and its temple is a related fellow mortal on a dying planet. Emily Brontë's literary brother in the enterprise of bearing the scriptural Jahweh and up-ending the Miltonic cosmos was Byron: 'brother' not 'father', for the stimulation of sharing common cause rather than the oppression of debt indicates her customary relish in acquisition. In 1833, when Emily was 15 years old, she had first read Byron's poetry and Moore's *Life of Byron*. His influence is often equated with the creation of the lawless, saturnine 'Byronic hero', a generally defiant turn of mind, and a taste for ill-fated lovers.[1] But Byron, especially in his 'Mystery Plays', *Cain* and *Heaven and Earth*, both of which elaborate themes in

Genesis, presented to her mind a critique of biblical orthodoxy which amounted to a religious vision. It challenged the religion of her father, and of the fathers in general. It drove the wedge of self-contradiction between God' power and God's love. It demonstrated that the Bible had slandered man by imputing the Father's crimes against his creatures to the fault of humanity. It proved the Almightly to be a disreputable parent, against whom it was fitting to protest.

The Byronic obsession with forbidden love, especially between brother and sister, entered Emily Brontë's imagination not solely as an exotic and erotic Romantic *topos* on which to nourish an adolescent fantasy, but as structuring an earthly alternative to the heavenly 'Love' whose logic she indicted. The question of literal incest, of course, does not arise directly in *Wuthering Heights*, since Heathcliff (though he suggestively inherits the name of a dead Earnshaw son) is and remains extraneous and malignant to the family interior: a changeling, gypsy, demon, 'out-and-outer' (p. 47), an 'it' speaking a foreign 'gibberish' (p. 35) whose seed is blight and who is ultimately extruded. Bersani's conviction that Heathcliff's advent into the family mimes the dilemma for an existing family presented by the birth of a new rival child, splitting the ambivalence of feelings generated by sibling-recognition between Catherine (passionate attachment) and Hindley (passionate hostility) is persuasive.[2] However, the text in a literal sense is overwhelmingly innocent of incestuous imputation. When, for instance, we conceive of Catherine's ' "resting her darling head on the same pillow"' with Heathcliff, the deep emotional tremor which accompanies the reader's glimpse into their most intimate privacy has no taint of sexual voyeurism: it is governed by the hallowing memory with which Heathcliff completes his

[margin note: But is he Earnshaw's illegit. son?]

93

sentence, '"*as she did when a child*"' (p. 290, emphasis added). Again, when Heathcliff disinters her corpse, the text is pure of Gothic innuendo. In thus tempering her Byronism to the austerities of her own literary mood, Emily Brontë's novel refuses assimilation to the knowingness which tends to characterise his accounts of brother-sister love. The nostalgic passion for the forbidden which she shares with Byron centres on a profane alternative to God which is lifted by the severe, dedicated fidelity of its protagonists to the level of the sacred and obligatory. *Wuthering Heights* is a world in which contrary principles fight for an unlimited allegiance; and allegiance once yielded can never be revoked. Allegiance is also, to some degree, tribal and genetic. Here, Byron's response to Genesis startlingly illuminates Emily Brontë's familial concerns. In a world of multiple antipathies, to bestow allegiance beyond the boundary of tribe is to risk swift or eventual fatal punishment. Byron's *Cain* and *Heaven and Earth* explore this tribal bonding, in a dualistic manner, in the light of a perception voiced by the patriarch Noah: 'Has not God made a barrier between earth/And heaven, and limited each to each, kind to kind' (*Heaven and Earth* I.iii.475-6).[3] The barrier between heaven and earth is echoed by the antipathy between the tribes of Cain and Seth, whose children innately reject one another:

> And dost thou think that we,
> With Cain's the eldest born of Adam's blood
> Warm in our veins,—strong Cain! who was begotten
> In Paradise,—would mingle with Seth's children?
> Seth, the last offspring of old Adam's dotage?
> No, not to save all earth, were earth in peril!
> (*Heaven and Earth* I.iii.388-95)

Lord David Cecil's famous formulation of *Wuthering*

Heights as the mating of 'children of storm' with 'children of calm'[4] might be rephrased in terms of Emily Brontë's Byronic inheritance as the intercourse between the children of Cain and those of Seth, with those of Cain imaginatively (and, in so far as imagination and morality coincide) even morally preferred by both authors. This licensing of Cain's children in *Cain* and *Heaven and Earth* and in *Wuthering Heights* generates a vigorous moral challenge to the code of Jahweh and the primitive ethics of Genesis. The Linton seed and the Linton creed resemble the obedient God-fearing tribe of Seth, preparing to sail out on the Ark across the Flood of indiscriminate divine wrath. The Earnshaw children of 'strong Cain...begotten in Paradise' have all the self-willed energy of the Byronic challengers to the Christian world-view. For us as readers of the book they also render an impression of electrifying beauty—'*these* beautiful/Children of Cain' (I.iii.350–1)—which is bound up both with the energetic sense of self they assert and also the challenge their aggressive innocence offers to the status quo. They hold in contempt the mild, the law-abiding and the humane:

> 'That is quite possible,' remarked Heathcliff, forcing himself to seem calm, 'quite possible that your master should have nothing but common humanity and a sense of duty to fall back upon. But do you imagine that I shall leave Catherine to his *duty* and *humanity*? and can you compare my feelings respecting Catherine, to his?...'
>
> (p. 148)

Here we are invited to choose between a passion destructively pure and monolithic and the gentle, tempered affections of a God-fearing Abel or Seth. To Heathcliff, the words *duty* and *humanity* are the hypocritical currency upon which society depends, a worth-

95

less issue, coined to debase emotion by bringing to play upon the person of the beloved values extrinsic to an allegiance without alloy. We partly accept that such words wrong Catherine; the novel persuades us that they are to the degree fallen and tainted in respect to her that they cannot take cognisance of the species, or tribe, to which her nature belongs. The reader has this knowledge because she or he is convinced of the essential unity and unanimity of Catherine and Heathcliff: that is to say, their likeness. This affinity is felt not only despite but, curiously, because of Heathcliff's changeling status within the family. His lack of attributable origins means that he could have come from literally anywhere. As the iron-filing flies to the magnet, with all the appearance of home-coming, so this item of human waste material on the streets of Liverpool gravitates to a father in Mr Earnshaw. In their 'tribal' resemblance, the children's unlikeness as male and female is apprehended as spurious. This theme is familiar in Byron. In *Manfred*, the hero tells the Witch of the Alps:

> She was like me in lineaments, her eyes,
> Her hair, her features, all, to the very tone
> Even of her voice, they said were like to mine...
> ...
> I loved her, and destroyed her...
>
> (II.ii.105-7, 117)

A salient difference in treatment of the motif lies in the fact that Emily Brontë's narrative omits to mirror externals in this way. Heathcliff and Catherine are not spoken of as bearing surface resemblance. To 'be' Heathcliff is hence not to impersonate Milton's Eve narcissistically loving her own face in the pool (*PL* IV.440-91)—though the second generation of blood-related cousins with their identical eyes are uncomfortably close to this condition. It is rather as we say that the lover of God in some sense mysteriously 'is' God.

In *Wuthering Heights* as in *Manfred*, tribal affinity is made to challenge the abyss of final absence. Manfred's address to the ghost of Astarte could be read as a commentary on *Wuthering Heights*:

> Hear me, hear me—
> Astarte! my beloved! speak to me:
> I have so much endured—so much endure—
> Look on me! the grave hath not changed thee more
> Than I am changed for thee.
> . . .
> Say . . . that I do bear
> This punishment for both—that thou wilt be
> One of the blessed—and that I shall die;
> For hitherto all hateful things conspire
> To bind me in existence—in a life
> Which makes me shrink from immortality—
> A future like the past. I cannot rest.
> I know not what I ask, nor what I seek.
> . . .
> Yet speak to me. . . .
> . . .
> Speak to me! I have wander'd o'er the earth,
> And never found thy likeness.
> . . .
> Speak to me! though it be in wrath;—but say—
> I reck not what—but let me hear thee once—
> This once—once more!
>
> (II. iv. 117–49)

Manfred's strongly charged incantation draws much of its hectic power to convey the pathology of a disturbed and churning personality *in extremis* from its obsessive doubling and trebling of individual words, and those words within repeated verbal patterns. 'I cannot rest' is its key. Its cyclical cries for two-in-one communion seem to present a language spectrally drained of meaning through incessant reiteration, rhythmically beating like an overcharged pulse.

The link is striking to Heathcliff's: '"Come in! come in!" he sobbed. "Cathy, do come. Oh do—*once* more! Oh! my heart's darling, hear me *this* time—Catherine, at last!"' (p. 27). Emily Brontë's habit of italicisation evidences her poetic concern for the rhythmic properties of highly wrought language as an essential constituent of fictional meaning. Maximising syllabic stress, she incorporates a pattern of verbal music not unlike the Celtic *cynghannedd*: stressed monosyllables bound with intricate assonantal and alliterative devices: m̲y h̲eart's darl̲ing, h̲ear m̲e. Typically the structure is a chiastic reversal. Italicisation indicates awareness of the fact that she could not (as Byron could) rely on the prosodic medium to achieve her effect for her. Clearly, she wanted it said this way, and no other. And she wanted the effect to be precisely that of the *Manfred* passage: his 'thee once/This once—once more' becomes her 'Oh do—*once* more'. For an author not notably given to literary allusion, the closeness of Emily Brontë's verbal debt to her source suggests a peculiar degree of emotiveness in that source, which would make her wish to duplicate the precise texture of the original. Such echoes of this key speech in fact occur throughout *Wuthering Heights*. They are present when Heathcliff tells of his interference with Catherine's grave in Volume 2, Chapter 15 ('"I saw her face again—it is hers yet"' [p. 288]; '"I could *almost* see her, and yet I *could not!*"' [p. 290]); his account of his sleeplessness and wanderings in search of her spirit (p. 290); his inability to die. The whole direction of his life is to enact what Byron's Nemesis defines:

> This is to be a mortal
> And seek the things beyond mortality.
> (II. iv. 158–9)

The extreme quality of the obsession appears to take its diabolical energy from the fact that the questor in both authors is engaged in a search not for a beloved other, but for a double, likeness, or other self.[5] In fact, it could be phrased as a quest for the self: a counterpart which fatedly and fatally offers a mirror identification, as the left hand mirrors the right. Each looks for a reflective symmetry upon the material of the world outside, which will come forward as one approaches it and identify itself as a validation of the individual life. As Catherine's mind begins to 'wander', she rambles back, sifting through time and space in search of her reflection. The years dissolve, place shifts, and she thinks she is at the Heights and the mirror is the black press, with a face in it. Nelly explains that there is no press.

> 'There is no press in the room, and never was'…
>
> 'Don't *you* see that face?' she enquired, gazing earnestly at the mirror.
>
> And say what I could, I was incapable of making her comprehend it to be her own; so I rose and covered it with a shawl.
>
> 'It's behind there still!… And it stirred. Who is it?…
>
> 'There's nobody here!… It was *yourself*, Mrs. Linton; you knew it a while since.'
>
> 'Myself… and the clock is striking twelve! It's true, then; that's dreadful!' (pp. 123–4)

In the obsessive search for a cloned double with whom to mate safely, Catherine has cast her reflection out upon the universe: her self is, to that degree, outcast. This exodus of her identity is angled back at us like a reflection in an answering mirror (and hence given

Emily Brontë

further aesthetic credibility) later in the book when the
whole of nature, like a gigantic numismatic surplus, is
seen by Heathcliff as imprinted with the icon of
Catherine (see pp. 155-6 below). To the degree that this
novel images to its readers a universe of catherines,
there *is* a face beind the concealing shawl. There is a
ghost at Lockwood's window. The child of Catherine is
Catherine, and the lover of Catherine is an extension of
Catherine. The effect of the text as a hall of mirrors is
aptly conveyed by the external narrator as he 'spells
over' the names he has read on the ledge of her window:
'a glare of white letters started from the dark, as vivid as
spectres—the air swarmed with Catherines' (p. 17).
Words here are less agents of denomination than
disintegrative codes to diffuse identity. Christian
names whose social function is to connote individuality
and surnames which distinguish tribe instead within
this riddling context cast refractions of 'Catherine' out
into a kind of void and unsubstantiated life ('spectral'
writing in the mind's eye, detached from source). In this
limbo of linguistic alienation, the familiar Romantic *topos*
of the sister-or-brother self is exposed as a potently
seductive threat to integration and survival. The novel
tests out the philosophy of Narcissus which the
adolescent Catherine spun out of her own entrails:
'"surely you, and every body have a notion that there is,
or should be, an existence of yours beyond you. What
were the use of my creation if I were entirely contained
here?"' (pp. 81-2). Its two fatal errors of reasoning ('is'
slides defensively into 'should be', and there is no
reason to impute a 'use' to creation) do not undermine
the allure of a philosophy which recalls elements of
Wordsworth, Byron and Shelley, especially the latter's
Epipsychidion in which another Emily, Emilia Viviani, is
twinned to the poet as a location of self: 'I am not thine: I
am a part of *thee*'.[6] However, *Wuthering Heights* tries for

something more than partiality—images of coalescence, fusion, transformation recur (see pp. 152-3 below)—and records a grander failure of the search for a self beyond the self. Catherine, toward the terminus of her brief life, arrives at the nightmare side of the image—the threshold upon which the Byronic heroes agonise, on which Heathcliff will survive for a full eighteen years—at the place of ghosts, shadows, doubles and duplicities. The self becomes a detachable shadow which might take on independent life. Heathcliff as a stray self, adrift, beyond the stability of time and place, is always in a sense the ghost of Catherine.

In the quest for reintegration, Catherine imagines herself back, deeper into childhood. The yearning is to recall and repair the initial act of severance which exiled the self into a Cainlike wandering from source:

> 'most strangely, the whole last seven years of my life grew a blank! I did not recall that they had been at all. I was a child; my father was just buried, and my misery arose from the separation that Hindley had ordered between me and Heathcliff—I was laid alone, for the first time, and rousing from a dismal doze after a night of weeping—I lifted my hand to push the panels aside, it struck the table-top! I swept it along the carpet and then memory burst in—my late anguish was swallowed in a paroxysm of despair—I cannot say why I felt so wildly wretched—it must have been temporary derangement, for there is scarcely cause—But supposing at twelve years old I had been wrenched from the Heights, and every early association, and my all in all, as Heathcliff was at that time, and been converted at a stroke into Mrs Linton, the lady of Thrushcross Grange, and the wife of a stranger; an exile, and outcast, thenceforth, from what had been my world—You may fancy a glimpse of the abyss where I grovelled!' (p. 125)

Wrenched from the Heights: the characteristically Miltonic energies with which Catherine's verb-founded language (especially in accounts of dream-states) figures extrusion declare the violent momentum of a fall from heaven. Pitched into the Miltonic 'abyss' (see pp. 58-9 above) Catherine impersonates the exiles and outcasts of Genesis: Lucifer, Eve, Cain, especially the latter. Her 'an exile, and outcast' recalls the agony of Cain as he responds to his Creator's stigmatisation of him as a 'fugitive and a vagabond':

> My punishment is greater than I can bear.
> Behold, thou hast driven me out this day from the face of the earth; and from they face shall I be hid; and I shall be a fugitive and a vagabond in the earth (Genesis 4 : 13-4)

Likewise, one of the two texts relevant to Jabes Branderham's demonic sermon of the 'Seventy Times seven' is Genesis 4:24 the homicide Lamech who is to be avenged 'seventy and sevenfold'.[7] Catherine's narrative of expulsion elides two consecutive separations into the one experience of disaster; as indeed they are aspects of the one fall. To be 'laid alone, for the first time' is for Catherine to encounter her grave: the excommunication of her first, secured self, as of one who unknowingly breaks a taboo and awakens to find herself a pariah. It is with this penalty in mind, the removal of her 'darling head' from the shared pillow, that we must read Heathcliff's later prodigious efforts to ensure that he and she will sleep together in the earth, so that ' "by the time Linton gets to us, he'll not know which is which!" ' (p. 288). This shared sleep in the one bed is the image of primordial security, the sharing of life at its most intimate, uninhibited and unconsciously trustful level. Hindley's separation of the two children (it is just at the age of adolescence) repeats the first great loss of union with the mother-world: the split into birth, weaning, the death of the mother and the transfer into the fathers' world. In other words, Catherine—by means of a familiar Romantic metaphor—is recording the riddle of man's and, more properly *woman's* ostracism from Eden and her sequestration in a postlapsarian world ('the lady of Thrushcross Grange'). As 'Mrs. Linton', shorn both of Christian name and patronymic, she takes up the estrangement of a Cainlike inheritance as 'the wife of a stranger'. *Stranger* in Emily Brontë is an evil word, perhaps the most hostile and intimidating in her entire vocabulary. 'Merciful was the decree that spared her', Charlotte wrote of her, 'when she was a stranger in a strange land', to let her die at home 'guarded' by her family.[8] Turned inside-out in a foreign world, this strong woman becomes a nakedly defenceless child, without bearings, incommunicado, looked through and through by the cold eyes of strangers. This is the level of deadly threat with which Catherine's two estrangements are loaded. In the quoted passage Hindley stands in for the Omnipotent, doing the Great Forbidder's work for him. Mr Earnshaw, the guarantor of her childhood liberties, is 'just buried': the elder brother assumes authority. In ordaining that Catherine shall live a cloven life, he effectively curses her. Yet Hindley is also God's chosen victim. His loss of Frances, Nelly's love for him as her 'twin', his distorted, aching love of Hareton, and his own and his son's degradation reveal him as another disinherited son of the Father.

Tribal affinity, and in particular the fraternal–sororal bond, are, both in Byron and in Emily Brontë, the basis of man's dispute with God: omnipotence has forbidden the fulfilment of man's and woman's deepest desires in androgynous union at source. In Byron, the original, innocent but illicit love is understood as overtly or covertly incestuous. The imaginative worlds of *The Bride of Abydos, Manfred, Cain* are lit with an aura of unspoken sexual crime. It is crucial to emphasise the extent to which the linguistic medium of *Wuthering Heights*, in all its versatility of texture and mood, austerely refrains from presenting forbidden secrets in this knowing light. Perhaps more than any other factor, this quality of honourable disinterestedness in the narrative opens out the experience uttered in Catherine and Heathcliff into an extenuated universality in which readers have confessed themselves able freely to share, even though the love represented on the page is an exclusive hoarding of intimate meaning. *Wuthering Heights* maintains as a standard of the holy (by reversing norms of perception) what *Manfred* betrays as a desperate lapse into the unholy (by inverting such norms). Hence Emily's deep echo of Manfred's Astarte-speech (see p. 97 above) is in part a contextual rebuke to Byron's cultivation of guilt: Heathcliff's '"Come in... Cathy, do come"' is guilt-free. The narrator draws off 'half angry to have listened at all' to that 'agony' (p. 27). We would speak less of 'illicit' than of 'disallowed' love in Emily Brontë, borrowing a term of her own: 'Relentless laws that disallow/True virtue and true joy below',[9] not because she is more discreet than Byron but because she is at once more plain-speaking and less subverted by conventional moral judgements. Byron's tone seems to relish the 'sin' of his protagonists; hers neither praises nor blames. She shares with Byron, however, a profound awareness of the sanctity and sanctuary of sister-brother love, and a perception of its retentive passion, disqualifying the lover from future adaptation to individuals beyond the family or tribe. The loyalties of childhood, their longevity and their status as a test for the quality of other emotion are a major theme of her poetry and prose:

But that pure light, changeless and strong,

> Cherished and watched and nursed so long;
> That love that first its glory gave
> Shall be my polestar to the grave.
>
> ('Now Trust a Heart', ll. 21–4)

> My sister! oh my sister!
> What were the world, or other worlds, or all
> The brightest future, without the sweet past—
> Thy love, my father's, all the life, and all
> The things which sprang up with me, like the stars
> Making my dim existence radiant with
> Soft lights which were not mine?
>
> (*Heaven and Earth* I.iii.433–9)

> Can this fond wish seem strange to me,
> To be what I have ever been?
> What other hath Zuleika seen
> From simple childhood's earliest hour?
>   What other can she seek to see
> Than thee, companion of her bower,
>   The partner of her infancy?
> These cherish'd thoughts with life begun
> . . .
> To meet the gaze of strangers' eyes
> Our laws, our creed, our God denies
>
> (*The Bride of Abydos* I.XIII. 418–25, 429–30)

Byron's exotic settings, in Turkey, or the Caucasus, or the desert outside Eden, are imported via Emily's Gondal (a mingling of stylish Mediterranean-sounding names and titles with a northern homeland) to the familial world of Penistone. In the rough beauty of Emily's well-rooted pastoral, the transplantation works metamorphosis of the original lurid material. The texture of the fibrous, peaty moorlands binds the 'partners of infancy' both in Gondal and more so in *Wuthering Heights* to a natural reality more resonant than anything in her imagination's brother. To Byron Emily Brontë adds Bewick. *Wuthering Heights* is a haunting meditation upon the relation of the child to the child of nature considered as the clutch of gravely observed lapwing-chicks exposed as corpses in their nest: '"we saw its nest in the winter, full of little skeletons"' (p. 122); the pair of nest-building ousels at the Grange (pp. 165–6); the dogs that lurk or bask in human habitations, and are thought worthy by the dispassionate author of being named and characterised; the puppies, excess to requirements, which Hareton is disclosed as hanging from a chair-back.

Because of this pastoral insistence on families of human beings as distinct species within a nature designated as a community of 'kind', to mate between families is made to appear a mismatch, though its offspring—harmonising contraries, as in the case of Hareton and the younger Catherine—may bring back renewed fertility to the original source, given a leaven of culture and affection. With a neat feminist reversal of Miltonic Adam's pedagogic pleasuring of Eve, 'solv[ing] high dispute/With conjugal caresses' (*PL*, VIII. 55–6), Catherine tames and civilises her cousin through the medium of linguistic acquirements: '"Con-*trary*! . . . That for the third time, you dunce!" (p. 307). To standardise a reading of *contrary* is on the face of it to reconcile the novel's polarities. Catherine's and Hareton's *coincidentia oppositorum* is, however, more conclusively a mating of kin with kin, like with like. The image of the first Catherine comes home to the likeness of Heathcliff. Nelly notes that they 'both appeared in a measure, my children' (p. 322) and observes, as does Heathcliff, to his ire and distress, that they have the same eyes, those of the elder Catherine. Hence the daughter of the first Catherine and the son of her brother unite within the house of origins to fulfill the yearning of the first generation, by proxy: the reassertion of the brother-sister bond. Part

Two of *Wuthering Heights*, which looks so tame, in fact reproduces more cunningly the subversions of Part One. Lockwood deliciously reinforces the Brontë prohibition on outsiders by continuing till the end to suppose that he might have captured the affections of the younger Cathy: 'I bit my lip, in spite, at having thrown away the chance I might have had, of doing something besides staring at [her] smiting beauty' (p. 308). The ineligible south has always the status of effete voyeur of the close-knit tribal north.

Hence the natural movement *out* of tribe to mate with a member of another is fatally unnatural in terms of preordained barriers and limits. Byronic and Brontean protagonists inhabit a closed system of contradictory logics, for if they mate within the tribe, as close to source as their natures dictate, their union generates a catastrophic alienation. The incest theme running through Byron's plays and narrative poems, from Manfred's love of Astarte, to *Cain* in which Cain and Adah, born 'on the same day, of the same womb' (I.i.328), share and transfer an inheritance of inexorable pain to the next generation, is organically linked with the Romantic denunciation of the God of Genesis. The preoccupation of *Cain* with original sin, and the ethical absurdity of the inheritance of a ruined and corrupted nature regardless of individual merit is also germane to *Wuthering Heights*. The novel inscribes its challenge to the Father-God as an implicitly feminist rebuke to the patrilinear and patriarchal disinheritance of woman and child. Responsibility for the unjust status quo is repeatedly thrust back upon the Maker, echoing Cain's assertion to Abel that 'thy God loves blood' (*Cain* III.i.310); equating the Maker with the Destroyer ('call him/Which name thou wilt', [*Cain* I.i.263–4]); identifying the predicament of man with that of all other sentient creatures who inherit a carnivorous universe of pain, as guiltless and guileless 'sad ignorant victims' (III.i.302).

Emily Brontë's repudiation of original sin is the crux on which her 'sinistral' theology is composed. Here loyalty to one's roots in childhood is focused not as a personal issue but as a theological commitment, which arouses in the language of desire and need on which I reflected in Chapters 1 and 2 a higher register of language of the spirit in which the fiction may address itself to the reader as a fellow child of God. Catherine, with pragmatic wickedness, writes her own story down the margins of a Testament. The story with which she invades the Good Book is not only a signal act of disobedience to the omniscient and omnipotent Author but a pointed comment on the value of his account of how things stand in the world. Her story in practice marginalises His, for of course the text of Emily Brontë's novel elects to reproduce only hers for us to read. *Wuthering Heights* as a whole works on a comparably blasphemous model, exhibiting the Scriptures as self-justifying fictions: it excitedly snatches the pen from the right hand of the Almighty and makes left-handed amendment for his stories' dubieties and inconsistencies. Its objection to the doctrine of original sin may be detected in the very modulations of its prose style: the curious absence of blame extended by the cool authorial tone to brutal actions—the most famous being that of Hareton 'who was hanging a litter of puppies from a chair-back in the doorway' (p. 181)—together with the quality of innocence which attaches to spectacular acts of wilful cruelty in the universe of the novel. Such behaviour has an aura of the predetermined; a post-lapsarian inevitability, for which individual members of the species can scarcely be held to blame. Hence, although a revenge-ethic dominates both the world of Gondal and that of *Wuthering Heights* ('Compassion reigns a little while/Revenge eternally'),[10] there is a paradoxical sense of the extension of full and free forgiveness on the part of the author. Through a combination of abstention from casting judgement on behaviour and the patent ineptitude of what narrative judgements are made, the author's characters are created, sustained and destroyed within the narrative equivalent of a communal state of Grace. This unique effect of cool charity originates in the stylising device of multiple narration and authorial abdication of the omniscient voice. Hence her characters accuse God and His Church with a degree of impunity comparable with those of Byronic drama—generically free from that evaluative partiality which traditionally typifies the novel—rebuked only by one another or by the busy tongue of Nelly, the servant of the story rather than its master.

The filthy, obscure and reprobated condition of natural man, tainted in the very seed of his being by an evil he did not personally approve—as taught by Luther and Calvin (see pp. 126–8 below) is most speakingly represented in the character of Heathcliff. He learns to wear his badge of exile as a blazon of courage: ' "I shall be as dirty as I please, and I like to be dirty, and I will be dirty" ' (p. 56). The narrative extension of Grace to him perfectly comprehends and communicates the origins of his desecrating pain. Flogged for throwing the hot apple sauce into Linton's face (p. 57), the child sits beside the fire leaning 'his two elbows on his knees, and his chin in his hands':

'I'm trying to settle how I shall pay Hindley back. I don't care how long I wait, if I can only do it, at last. I hope he will not die before I do!'

'For shame, Heathcliff!' said I. 'It is for God to punish wicked people; we should learn to forgive.'

'No, God won't have the satisfaction that I shall,' he returned. 'I only wish I knew the best way! Let me alone, and I'll plan it out: while I'm thinking of that, I don't feel pain.' (p. 60)

'We should learn to forgive': the inadequacy of Nelly's response to Heathcliff's intense distress, requiring the morphine of enmity, is implied by its taking the character of irony, sandwiched as it is between Heathcliff's two lacerated expositions of his remedy for his own rejection. The vivid detail with which Emily Brontë invests these crucial scenes of abuse (the apple sauce, the boy's gloomy posture) reinforces a reader's sense of the inevitability of the vicious process of reprobation into which Heathcliff's existence has been precipitated. It is thus that *we* learn the lesson which must be lost on Heathcliff: 'We should learn to forgive'. Forgiveness in this sense is a literary act coerced from us by the character of the imaginative world into which *Wuthering Heights'* children have fallen. The moral acknowledgement which Emily Brontë's book induces us to make is not dissimilar to that elicited from the Byronic Cain by Lucifer:

> *Luc.*   What does thy God love?
> *Cain.*   All things, my father says; but I confess
>   I see it not in their allotment here.
>
>   (II.ii.310-12)

It is the 'allotment' made by God to man which *Wuthering Heights* invites us to judge rather than man himself: to test for ourselves whether what 'my father says' to justify God's ways to men can be a correct or adequate account.

The problem of original sin is as central to the work of Emily Brontë as it is to Byron: it is considered to be the most flagrant breach of logic and morality committed by the Creator in respect to his creatures. Cain's lament over the future of his sleeping baby recalls Milton's epitaph over the future of the sleeping Adam and Eve in the frail safety of their Edenic bower: 'Sleep on/Blest pair.... And know to know no more' (IV.773–5):

> He smiles, and sleeps! Sleep on,
> And smile, thou little, young inheritor
> Of a world scarce less young: sleep on, and smile!
> ...
> Thou know'st not thou art naked...
>
>   Ay! dream of [Paradise]
> My disinherited boy! 'Tis but a dream;
> For never more thyself, thy sons, nor fathers,
> Shall walk in that forbidden place of joy!
>
> Little deems our young blooming sleeper there,
> The germs of an eternal misery
> To myriads is within him! better 'twere
> I snatch'd him in his sleep, and dash'd him 'gainst
> The rocks, than let him live to—
> (*Cain* III.i.18–20; 23; 31–4; 122–6)

The baby is seen and known by his natural father as innocent; in the eyes of the supernatural (and hence unnatural) Father in heaven he is already contaminated by a corruption born with him into the world. Cain's lullaby over Enoch is an elegy. To be born outside Paradise is to register as an eternal outcast and outsider, regardless of deserts. Hence Childhood, from which the most sacred loyalties spring, is a false Eden. Cain emphasises the infant's entire vulnerability in the light of a foreknown future; and the implanted taint within the child's loins, his curse on future generations. The remembrance of Psalm 137 (the dashing of the 'little ones' of Babylon against the stones) ranks the indefensible child with the waste human material to be

111

eliminated by divine wrath. When we come upon the
following conversation in *Wuthering Heights*, we are
aware that the stigma borne by the children of Cain is
already transcribed on the forehead of the novel's
children:

> 'Come, come, be merry, and like yourself! Look at
> Hareton—*he's* dreaming nothing dreary. How sweetly he
> smiles in his sleep!'
> 'Yes; and how sweetly his father curses in his solitude!
> You remember him, I dare say, when he was just such
> another as that chubby thing—nearly as young and
> innocent' (p. 79)

This passage is clearly directly related to Cain's requiem
for doomed childhood, 'He smiles, and sleeps', which in
turn focuses its vision of innocence back through a
jaundiced glass to Milton's 'blest pair' sleeping together
in Paradise. As Byron judges the God of Judgment for
His outlandish behaviour in relation to such speaking
images of vulnerability, so *Wuthering Heights* sardonically
reflects on the bequest which is (however involuntarily)
willed from father to son, from generation to generation. Each is concerned with inheritance, the 'germs of
misery' which are transferred in the act of procreation.
Catherine inadvertently touches upon the deep childish
life of Nelly in her kinship with Hindley: '"You
remember him, I dare say...."' Two chapters later, we
are fleetingly to share Nelly's activated memory of 'my
early playmate seated on the withered turf, his dark,
square head bent forward, and his little hand scooping
out the earth with a piece of slate' (p. 108). The novel
presses without remorse upon the bruise of the
question: how did the child come to fall so heavily into
the emergency of adult life? Catherine's speech skirts
this question without direct engagement. But the dream

which she wants to impart to Nelly, and which Nelly does not want to hear, involves a direct refusal of divine standards of behaviour, which the novel seems to probe as it enacts its own stealthy demolition of Christian ethics, theology and the very architecture of the Church itself. It is the dream in which ' "heaven did not seem to be my home" ' (p. 80), exasperating the angels to such a pitch that they eject Catherine on to the heath at the Heights where ' "I awoke sobbing for joy" '. This abuse of divine hospitality reveals a flaw in the divine plan whereby the angelic faces, taking on the aspect of demons in relation to her, prove her worst suspicions founded: heaven is a false, inimical home in which there exist no mirroring likenesses of Catherine's self. The angels in her dream are no kin to her, their filial allegiance to the Father–Creator being antagonistic to her attachment to the mother–creation.

In the ruin and reclamation of Hareton, the last of the 'H' coded male Heights characters, Emily Brontë works through her dramatisation of the nightmare of the Fall to an intimation of a *Paradise Regained* which reverses both Genesis and Milton by predicating re-entry to Eden on conjunction with the feminine soul-mate. In a diagrammatically coded novel such as *Wuthering Heights*, where identity gives the illusion not only of doubling but of trebling, and recurring in new permutations of the original raw materials (Linton–Heathcliff, Hindley–Heathcliff–Hareton, Catherine I and II), it can seem less decorous to speak of the artist's characterisation of individuals than of relatedly named characters as ciphering human nature, elaborating areas of being. This is related to the sense of universality recorded by readers: our intuition that human nature is in some cryptic manner abstracted on the page before us, sharing between configurations of identity the subliminal common material out of which human character is composed. Hence the configuration Heathcliff–Hindley –Hareton presents a reading of human nature which is in some way *prior* to individuation, just as their ethical world may be read as pre-moral (see p. 81 above). The replication of Heathcliff's fall in Hindley is repeated in Hareton, the former's foster-son and the latter's son. But the confirmation such patterns imply of the inevitability of original sin is criticised by *Wuthering Heights'* emphasis on conditioning as a crucial source of behaviour, warp to the weft of genetic inheritance, in response to which individual character modulates toward its fullest possibility of Grace or degradation: '"Now, my bonny lad, you are *mine!*"' Heathcliff sneers at Hareton, '"And we'll see if one tree won't grow as crooked as another, with the same wind to twist it!"' (p. 186). Such an organic analogy allows for the possibility of hale growth, given good soil, clement weather and nurture, which is in effect what Hareton receives in the remedial therapy of love received from Catherine in the second part of the novel. Through the pivotal character of Hareton, the novel expounds a myth of recovery for the ruined 'H' characters which belongs neither to 'Heaven' nor 'Hell' but is earth-born and earth-bounded.

The association of Hareton with original sin is explicitly symbolised in the chapter in which Nelly, at a crossroads, dreams awake of the child Hindley, and goes to seek him at the Heights, finding instead his son 'Hareton, *my* Hareton', looking through the bars of the gate (p. 109). The substitution of child for child reinforces the cyclically repetitive theme of the mass reiteration of the curse on Adam. '"How sweetly his father curses in his solitude!"' Cathy had observed over the sleeping baby. The first words Nelly hears from 'the stammering lips of the little fellow' are 'a string of curses' (p. 109). This duplication of father and son gives an impression of universality to the state of betrayal in which they are implicated. After the curses comes physical violence, the sin of Cain: Hareton hurls a large flint at Nelly, who takes 'an orange from my pocket', which the child snatches 'as if he fancied I only intended to tempt and disappoint him'. The offer of *tempting, disappointing* fruit is loaded with significance in this post-Edenic world of the fathers in which (though only ten months exiled from feminine care) Hareton has already fallen into an almost unrecognisable condition:

'Who's your master?'
   'Devil daddy,' was his answer.
   'And what do you learn from Daddy?' I continued.
   He jumped at the fruit; I raised it higher. 'What does he teach you?' I asked.
   'Naught,' said he, 'but to keep out of his gait—Daddy cannot bide me, because I swear at him....
   '...he pays Dad back what he gies to me—he curses Daddy for cursing me—He says I mun do as I will.' (pp. 109–10)

Nelly is only exploiting the fruit, to manipulate the already fallen child into divulging the knowledge she needs. The dialogue with its reiterated chant of 'Dad... Daddy... Devil daddy' reveals a strange moral equivalence between the two parties within whose bitter personal quarrel the child is ammunition. Both 'Devil daddy' (Heathcliff) and 'Daddy' (Hindley) speak the language of the curse; are apprehended as shadowy, fratricidal alter egos bound to a course of mutual annihilation. The child's mouthings of the bad language inherited from his twin fathers, echoes the novel's frequent equation of God the Father with Satan the Adversary, as exemplifications of an identical evil.

*   *   *

In the Scriptures, redemption is worked for man by the mediatorial Son of the Father. In Emily Brontë's heretical reversal of paternal traditions, it is achieved by reincorporation within the daughter of the mother. *Wuthering Heights* is remarkable for the uxoriousness of its male protagonists: Heathcliff's passion for Catherine is paralleled by Linton's, Hindley's for Francis, Hareton's for the second Catherine. The thwarting of these primal allegiances—a love which worships its idolised object as a version of God—represents the exile from Paradise. Hence, what is sin in Milton is virtue in Emily Brontë. The principle of likeness between male and female in the matrix of familial bonding is perhaps the supremely anti-Miltonic stance held by *Wuthering Heights*. Milton's stern insistence on sexual inequality is grounded in the logic of innate and nearly invariable differentiation and specialisation. Difference is the basis of caste:

> both
> Not equal, as their sex not equal seemed;
> For contemplation he and valour formed,
> For softness she and sweet attractive grace;
> He for God only, she for God in him:
> His fair large front and eye sublime declared
> Absolute rule....
>
> (IV.295–301)

Wuthering Heights scrambles Milton's class-riddled gender terminology. It is the gentle, tenderly possessive Edgar Linton who plays the role of the Miltonic woman— formed for 'softness' ('The soft thing' [p. 72], a 'sweet, low manner of speaking' [p. 69]) and 'sweet attractive grace'. Nelly holds the candle to his picture for Lockwood:

> I discovered a soft-featured face, exceedingly resembling the young lady at the Heights, but more pensive and

amiable in expression. It formed a sweet picture. The long light hair curled slightly on the temples; the eyes were large and serious; the figure almost too graceful. I did not marvel how Catherine Earnshaw could forget her first friend for such an individual. I marvelled much how he, with a mind to correspond with his person, could fancy my idea of Catherine Earnshaw. (p. 66)

Soft, amiable, sweet, graceful are all Miltonic words of modified approval recurrently associated with the feminine in *Paradise Lost*.[11] Linton is visually lovely, created to attract, temptingly beautiful to Catherine, and quiescent where she is all animation and vital force. Though he qualifies as 'contemplative', he lacks the Miltonic (and Earnshaw) 'valour' which the author herself possessed to an heroic degree. Even Linton's hair is the Miltonic prototype for femininity: long, curling and fair. His role as magistrate impersonates an 'Absolute rule' he is constitutionally unfitted to fulfil: Linton brings in men with cudgels when he wishes to assert control, for he has not—within himself— authority.

Charlotte drew attention to Emily's resistance to the institutionalised doubled standards of morality for men and women which their society took on trust: her contempt for 'any insinuation that the faithfulness and clemency, the long-suffering and loving-kindness which are esteemed virtues in the daughters of Eve, become foibles in the sons of Adam'.[12] In *Wuthering Heights* we witness a wholesale transference of these qualities from gender to tribe, without devaluation, in the person of Linton. The Linton gentleness is accepted into *Wuthering Heights* with a sort of awe at the unchanging beauty of its fidelity to its own principles and its inexhaustible attachment to both Catherines. Edgar's adoration of the first Catherine is the 'love of youth' as well as

Heathcliff's—not as long-standing as the latter's (if we descend to the calculation of years) and without the semblance of familial propinquity, but early and exclusive. Near his death he remembers himself: 'musing by myself among those stones, under that old church—lying, through the long June evenings, on the green mound of her mother's grave, and wishing, yearning for the time when I might lie beneath it' (p. 257). To lie 'on the green mound of her mother's grave' is to interpret into verbal music of a clement pastoral the savage urgency of Heathcliff's desire to enter the grave and compose his nature into the substance of Catherine's death. In each case allegiance to an earth which incorporates the beloved mother-sister-wife-friend is primary and final. The melodic poise of Linton's sentence in a chiasmus of sound—green: mound:: mother's: grave—shapes his passion in terms of the harmony of a character rooted in the fertile natural cycle. Ultimately, Catherine's grave centralises those of Linton and Heathcliff: the warring tribes of Seth and Cain concur at either side of the self to whom each refers, exemplifying to eternity the same virtue: fidelity. The 'feminine' Linton and the 'masculine' Heathcliff are equally exemplary in this virtue, like fraternal twins, light and shadowy.

Hence, Emily Brontë's joyous literary feud with Milton is conducted not just through the Church-hating, God-daring passion of Catherine and Heathcliff, but—more straightforwardly, through the God-fearing Edgar Linton's preference for the religion of human love over the religion of his fathers. Adam's failing (the overvaluing of Eve) is read in *Wuthering Heights* as both Heathcliff's *and* Linton's redemptive virtue:

'with thee
Certain my resolution is to die;

How can I live without thee, how forgo
Thy sweet converse and love so dearly joined,
To live again in these wild woods forlorn?
Should God create another Eve, and I
Another rib afford, yet loss of thee
Would never from my heart; no no, I feel
The link of nature draw me: flesh of flesh,
Bone of my bone thou art, and from thy state
Mine never shall be parted, bliss or woe.'

(PL IX.906–16)

Adam's 'so absolute she seems/And in her self complete'
(VIII.547–8) is scowlingly reprimanded by the otiose
Archangel. Adam's abandonment of the statutes of the
Father for loyalty to his need of inseparable human kin
(Eve is both his offspring and his wife) is the blasphemy
which ruins him and entails the loss of his home. In
Wuthering Heights values are reversed. To have denied Eve
this priority would have been the profane aberration.
The first Catherine's characteristics cluster in the
traditional archetype of the sinning Eve—headstrong
disobedience, an eloquent and vagrant tongue, self-will,
changefulness, irrationality, a witching beauty and the
power to dream. 'Was she they God?' the 'sovereign
presence' might jealously have enquired—of Linton and
Heathcliff as of Milton's Adam (PL X.145)—an interrogation to which each must have replied, proudly, 'She
was and is'. The single allegiance of immemorial enemies
is figured in their kin deaths: Heathcliff on the one side
and Edgar Linton on the other, dying with 'eyes that
seemed dilating with ecstasy', a 'rapt, radiant gaze'
(p. 284). The displacement of heaven made by *Wuthering
Heights* from the supernatural to the natural, the Father's
transcendence to the mother's immanence, heightens to
the state of worship the religious attitude displayed in
Emily Brontë's poetry: the yearning to close one's eyes
on the world of loss and exile and 'waken but to share

with thee/A mutual immortality' (see pp. 40–1 above).
Both Linton and Heathcliff, in making an eager and
idolatrous participation in Catherine's death echo
Adam's pledge to Eve—'with thee/Certain my resolution
is to die' mutually affirming 'The link of nature'
distrusted by Milton. The narrator inscribes upon their
dying eyes the appearance of a beatitudinous vision
never associated by the novel with orthodox or
institutionalised Christianity; in fact severely dis-
sociated from it, as if to reiterate the vatic dismissal of
religious dogmas as 'Vain... unutterably vain... worth-
less... idle' in 'No coward soul'.

To read *Wuthering Heights* alongside Scripture and
Milton is to interpret a prose fiction within the generic
tradition of sacred poetry. Genre, as Kermode reminds
us, is the first of the 'constraints that shadow
interpretation'.[13] However, Emily Brontë, through the
very obliquity and interiority of her fiction, opens out
the genre of the novel to radical assessment. Several
factors in *Wuthering Heights* imply a modulation of Emily
Brontë's poetic narrative toward the condition of
narrative poetry; however, other (frequently noted)[14]
factors are generically suggestive of poetic drama. Both
novels and narrative poetry are commonly governed by
a normative standard of judgement ('So spake the false
dissembler', 'So glozed the Tempter, and his proem
tuned' [*PL* III.681; IX.549]), of which *Wuthering Heights* is
free. Instead of dialogue, this novel often presents a
series of internally coherent and poetically powerful
'speeches'—sometimes in the form of semi-soliloquy
(Ch. 12), choric, inspirational (Ch. 9, pp. 79–82) or
invocatory and ritualistic (Vol. 2, Ch. 1). We are naturally drawn to read and interpret these speech-
sequences as if we were reading closet drama: Milton's
Samson or Byron's *Cain*. Jacobean drama is often cited as
parallel material, but the language of *Wuthering Heights*

has a peculiarly *silent* eloquence, belonging to the act of solitary reading on the page rather than to the theatre of communal exchange. It is a curious fact that the material of these 'speeches' when read aloud fails to impress the ear as it did the mind: we are reading, then, a profoundly introverted, scripted and anonymous drama. Disparate voices participate in the one choric rhetoric of desire, recording a passion raised to a power so high that it realises itself only in the strange purity and character-less blankness of words-on-the-page. If Catherine and Heathcliff are one, they also speak the one language. It is as ritualised as that of Greek tragic art, but whereas in Greek the informing myths and meanings are known as those of the whole community, in Emily Brontë the secret mysteries readers sense within the formulaic speech-patterns and are consumed with curiosity to share, are intimate hoardings within the text.

To focus, however, on the Byronic 'Mystery Plays' makes it possible for us to address that area of *Wuthering Heights* which utters itself as ritual of occult communion between soul which affirm their sacred secrets in our hearing, like the Eleusinian revelation of *ta hiera* before the witnessing initiates. We do not undertake this in order to demythologise the arcanely private inwardness of the novel's central mystery (the novel has always mocked code-breakers) but to estimate the oblique angle of its spiritual energies in relation to the author's Christian inheritance. To read the chapter which relates the last meeting between Catherine and Heathcliff alongside Byron's *Heaven and Earth* in terms of the dramatic 'speeches' which articulate their mutual commitment and rebuke, is to register the ritualistic address which translates a language of impiety and transgression into a code of allegiance, with an austere *credo* and a severe ethic of its own. The energy which animates this language of demonic communion, so that

121

readers of all persuasions are prepared to receive it as an aspect of the holy, originates in its power to shock. Shock is then converted to awe at the dedication of the protagonists to the intrinsic logic and ideality of their bond, their ruthless commitment to the strictures of a personal law. Their heart-shaken utterance of extreme mutual pain, failure and loss (which was my subject in Ch. 1) then dissolves the reader's possible estrangement from the heresy of pure egoism in a sense of the inalienably human. While the narrative line holds fast to its duty to describe, rationalise, ironise where it can and confess the difficulty of interpretation, the 'speeches' ritualise a reversal of Christian belief whereby Heathcliff can present himself as an abstract of Virtue, entitled to turn his back upon God in moral indignation. His outburst against Cathy's breaking of faith is a classic declaration of *saeva indignatio*:

> 'You teach me now how cruel you've been—cruel and false. *Why* did you despise me? *Why* did you betray your own heart, Cathy? I have not one word of comfort—you deserve this. You have killed yourself. Yes, you may kiss me, and cry; and wring out my kisses and tears. They'll blight you—they'll damn you. You loved me—then what *right* had you to leave me? What right—answer me—for the poor fancy you felt for Linton? Because misery, and degradation, and death, and nothing that God or Satan could inflict would have parted us, *you*, of your own will, did it. I have not broken your heart—*you* have broken it—and in breaking it, you have broken mine. So much the worse for me, that I am strong. Do I want to live? What kind of living will it be when you—oh God! would *you* like to live with your soul in the grave?' (p. 161)

Heathcliff's testament bears clear relation to the love speech of Aholibamah to her Seraph-lover in Byron's *Heaven and Earth*:

> But thee and me he never can destroy;
> Change us he may, but not o'erwhelm; we are
> Of as eternal essence, and must war
> With him if he will war with us: with *thee*
> I can share all things, even immortal sorrow;
> For thou hast ventured to share life with *me*,
> And shall I shrink from thine eternity?
> No! though the serpent's sting should pierce me
> thorough,
> And thou thyself wert like the serpent, coil
> Around me still! and I will smile,
> And curse thee not; but hold
> Thee in as warm a fold
>
> (I.i.119–30)

Heathcliff's enraged lament is for the breaking of such a dangerous, secure trust as this between woman and angel (equals and likenesses, engaged in the same 'war' against the Almighty's jealous potency). His casual contempt for conventional standards of morality exists in the context of a world for him outrageously disordered from the first, as in Byron's vision of God as the Creator–Destroyer, named by mortals as 'the implacable Omnipotent' (I.iii.860) whose creation's catastrophic suffering reflects to his eternal discredit. Misery, degradation, death, God, Satan are itemised in a roll-call of enemies to be resisted by the 'eternal essence' of incorporate human nature. The collapse of the distinction between 'God' and 'Satan', together with the ascription of negligible value to the pair of them, is contingent upon Catherine's and Heathcliff's relocation of the theatre of meaning, from the outer universe to the interior cosmos. Since the primal allegiance is to one another, the entire religious lexicon has to be revised. It would be wrong to claim that Heathcliff and Catherine act or speak without regard for morality, law and religious imperative. On the contrary, the quoted speech dwells wholly on the authority of language connoting sacramental truth and ethical obligation. It is concerned with Cathy's 'sin' as the forsaking of human allegiance; with 'damnation' as the inner torment consequent upon such abdication. 'What *right* had you to leave me?': mutual identification has the primacy of law. This inner world is envisaged as a sanctuary which seals in to its integral safety the mutually confirming twin egos, in a capsule which immunises against the pain of the postlapsarian world ('misery'); denies the relevance of the fall itself ('degradation'); and scorns the mortality of the body. This combined resistance to external stress leaves the psyche susceptible only to one threat—of self-division—but against that fact, it is more powerless than any child. ' "Would *you* like to live with your soul in the grave?" ' A visually commanding total of six italicisations propels the passage along through a course of moral outrage which seeks ungovernably to register the fact of the sacrilegious breaking of a taboo. Catherine's response composes itself into a ritual acknowledgement of her friend's reading of her separation from him as a fall from Grace: ' "I forgive you. Forgive me" ' (p. 161).

Byron's *Heaven and Earth* had dramatised the mating together of seceding angels and human women in Genesis 6: 'the sons of God saw the daughters of men that they were fair; and they took them wives of all which they chose', quoting a motto from Coleridge's *Kubla Khan*, 'And woman wailing for her demon lover', a poem which demonstrably finds an echo in Emily's 'The Philosopher's Conclusion'. Byron's angels prefer their allegiance to mortal woman to that which they owe to God, choosing the contempt of their kind and alienation from the Father rather than the hell of separation from their beloved partners. The flagrant breach of protocol on the part of Byron's female protagonist, in the quoted speech, includes blasphemy against Christ's incarnation:

'thou hast ventured to share life with *me*' is spoken not to an authorised Messiah but to a daemonic lover, a Seraph who is as brazenly welcomed as Eve welcomed the Serpent, to 'pierce me through' and 'coil/Around me' in sexual possession. Daemonic possession bears erotic implications in several of Emily Brontë's lyric poems concerning creativity ('I'll come when thou art saddest', the 'He comes with western winds' section of 'Julian M. and A.G. Rochelle'). Byron's salaciousness, however, is wholly avoided. In Emily Brontë the daemonic male Muse is always ultimately part of the self,[15] and in *Wuthering Heights* (as 'heath', as 'cliff', as a child without a surname) he is both grounded in the sentient clay of the familiar earth and rooted in our common childhood. Whereas Byron's Seraphs are the Father's dissident sons, Emily Brontë's Heathcliff, equally with Catherine, displays the signature of the mother.

Chapter Four

Father-God, Mother Earth

A Language of Rejection

The bizarre religious joy which characterises *Wuthering Heights*—a joy in the pure mania of religious fanaticism, celebrating the sublime insanity of Jehovah and His prophets—belongs not to a vestigial Romantic Satanism but to the mainstream radical Protestant tradition. The wrath of a punitive Old Testament, Apocalyptic and Lutheran God is drawn repeatedly into the text and converted with the greatest relish into violent linguistic energy. Luther and Calvin, whose inheritance both of language and of world-view the Brontë children had received at the hands of their Calvinistic Methodist Aunt Branwell, had explicitly gloried in the inhumane behaviour of their God, as recorded in Scripture and in history, as appealing not to human reason but to 'blind faith':

Thus God hides his eternal goodness and mercy under

eternal wrath, his righteousness under iniquity. This is the highest degree of faith, to believe him merciful when he saves so few and damns so many, and to believe him righteous when by his own will he makes us necessarily damnable, so that he seems, according to Erasmus, to delight in the torments of the wretched and to be worthy of hatred rather than of love.

It is likewise the part of this incarnate God to weep, wail, and groan over the perdition of the ungodly, when the will of the Divine Majesty purposely abandons and reprobates some to perish. And it is not for us to ask why he does so, but to stand in awe of God who both can do and wills to do such things.[1]

The tone of Luther's justification of God's immorality and absurdity (as judged by the eye of human Reason) can only be described as a kind of malign relish. He does far more than admit to the absurdity of Scripture: he is well pleased to assert and applaud it.[2] This Lutheran and Calvinist willingness to dance on the graves of the damned, and to signal God's wholesale reprobation of the majority of His children for no assignable reason, is an essential element of the Protestantism with which Emily Brontë's childish eye was greeted as consciousness dawned in her father's house. It was a language of rejection and ejection, whose edict enforced upon her the duty to love a hateful God. It was represented as a severe test of one's election that one be able to believe—through the efficacy of Faith and Grace to overturn the insistences of reason and human standards of decency—that what we humans interpret as sheer wickedness becomes, when attributed to the Deity, unquestionable evidence of Goodness. Even Luther acknowledged that he had experienced difficulty in accepting this offensive logic.[3] But once an individual had learnt to believe the unbelievable and to credit the discreditable, a marvellous sense of liberation overcame the privileged spirit.

Emily Brontë was brought up in a Dissenting area rooted in the eighteenth-century Evangelical Revival.[4] Haworth was the hellfire preacher William Grimshaw's old parish, a port of call for John Wesley in 1761 ('What hath God wrought in the midst of these rough mountains!')[5], whose chapels had been the frequent scene of uproar and riot. *Wuthering Heights* exemplifies the godly community in the predestinarian ranter, Joseph, shadowed by his dream-double 'Jabes Branderham', himself a fictionalised shadow of the Wesleyan Jabez Bunting against whom the Brontë family harboured a grudge for putting their uncle out of a job.[6] The godly man in *Wuthering Heights* is characterised by insanity of a grotesque and unruly kind, associated with physical and verbal violence and given to speaking a choicely inscrutable dialect of hatred and threat. The godly man is misogynistic, patriarchal, caste-bound and of rancorous humour. His chief antagonist is womankind, both in the persons of two generations of Catherines and in the narrative voice of Nelly, who never has a good word to say for him. Joseph speaks for his God in epitomising the language of rejection which characterises the pitiless Calvinist Deity. But as a comic figure—surely *the* comic figure of the novel—he also focuses the novel's saturnalian impulse to scourge authority and bring low the Mighty. In discharging against Joseph volleys of linguistic energy as scornful laughter, the author permits us stealthy licence to mock the Author of Creation by making (in a classically Aristotelean comic alignment) his only representative and spokesman in the text a comic figure who stands lower than the reader. The Babel utterances of a manic servant disclose the possible fallacy of every sacred Truth he utters.

Wuthering Heights suggests to the present reader that

Emily Brontë saw essentially the same God as Luther's, one who hides his 'righteousness under iniquity', but that in interpreting his works with the cold eye of Reason (which Luther had anathematised as 'blind, deaf, stupid, impious, and sacrilegious'),[7] she doubly judged Him: first, as opprobious; second, as ridiculous. Irony in *Wuthering Heights* conveys, amongst other things, a religious attitude, fiercely relishing the enormities of the Father who mocks his own creatures with such a curious mixture of sanctimoniousness and barbarity, and measuring the gap between man's claims for the Goodness of God and the loveless universe in which humanity finds itself. The ironic gap is as vast as the 'abyss' recurrently alluded to (see pp. 58–9 above). The savage humour animating the novel often expresses itself in virtuoso outbursts of cantankerous mutiny against the Creator on the part of the book's children: Hindley inveighs against the tyranny of his circumstances, and when invited by Nelly to have mercy on his own soul, replies, '"Not I! on the contrary, I shall have great pleasure in sending it to perdition, to punish its maker," exclaimed the blasphemer. "Here's to its hearty damnation!"' (p. 75). There is a special flair in the prose in which Emily Brontë's characters defy or deny the Almighty, conceiving a swaggering glory in turning back his own punitive laws against the Creator. The narrative vicariously enjoys the power to 'exclaim' as 'the blasphemer' through the mouth of Hindley, to impersonate, as it were, the child who finds the way to punish its parent by threatening to hurt itself, as Hindley does here. The novel's retaliatory energy is exemplified in the first Cathy's account in her childish diary of her hurling of pious literature into the dog-kennel: '"Maister, coom hither! Miss Cathy's riven th'back off 'Th'Helmet uh Salvation,' un' Heathcliff's pawsed his fit intuh t' first part uh 'T' Brooad Way to Destruction!"' (p. 19). The full armour of God is as frail as paper: Catherine rips the jacket off her tract and Heathcliff kicks his to pieces. We hear Joseph's announcement of this demolition-work with unfeigned delight. The phonetic meticulousness of the novel's taking of dictation—like a devastatingly efficient secretary—reinforces the reader's participation in the communal orgy of destruction: for a tract entitled 'The Broad Way to Destruction' may be marginally amusing, but to widen the girth of the word to 'Brooad Way' has a savour of glory. In this way, the text's comic voice ensures our concurrence with anarchy and our sympathy for the unholy alliance of the naughty children as against the anarchic religiosity of the unholy old man. Into this climate of retaliation against the Spiritual Powers even Lockwood, the outsider, (albeit in his sleep) is drawn:

> 'Seventy times seven times have I plucked up my hat and been about to depart—Seventy times seven times have you preposterously forced me to resume my seat. The four hundred and ninety-first is too much. Fellow martyrs, have at him! Drag him down, and crush him to atoms, that the place which knows him may know him no more!
>
> (p. 22)

The text of Lockwood's dream is an intricate mesh of biblical texts concerned with God's designation of the unholy man, indicted as a taboo-breaker and punished by extrusion from the fold.[8] The inflammation of Lockwood's brain with a boredom 491 times too infernal for human nature to abide, parallels the excoriation of the children's nerves on their 'awful Sunday!' (p. 18) and issues in the same violent impulse to ensure that villainous piety should take a fall, and good discourse be thrown to the Devil, or the dog. It would be hard for the virtuous reader to decline the novel's open invitation to join in the fray, on the side of Antichrist, encouraging

the disreputable rabble of God's congregation to turn
the chapel into a place of riot, resonant with 'rappings
and counter-rappings' in which 'Every man's hand was
against his neighbour' (p. 22) as hard as to desire the
errant children to stay in with the detestable Sabba-
tarian rather than exodus for 'a scamper on the moors'
under the shelter of the dairywoman's cloak.

The language in which Lockwood's dream participates
is a rhetoric of eviction and demolition. His counter-
blast against Jabes exactly mirrors the Puritan oratory
of that sage. *Drag him down*, orders Lockwood's dream-
persona, moved by 'sudden inspiration' to assume the
authority of the Elect with which to eject the reprobated
minister on the grounds of causing insupportable
longueur. *'Thou art the Man!'* ripostes Jabes, and rouses the
saints to pulverise the yawning apostate. This dream-
episode represents a narrative interpretation of the
foreign gibberish of inexplicable signs which Lockwood
has encountered on penetrating Wuthering Heights—
the upside-down misanthropist's heaven in which dogs
reverse God in taking pride of place, the prime desire of
the snarling human hosts is to bundle the visitor out into
the snow even if it kills him, and the bedroom swarms
with odd messages of unknown Catherines. *Our*
interpretation of the interpolated dreams in *Wuthering
Heights* is likely to be parabolic to the novel as a whole.[9]
With exceptional clarity (just because it is cast in the
form of a dream) the Jabes episode exemplifies the
dynamic of the novel as a dualistic contention, a
powerful charge of energy running both ways at once,
stemming from the quarrel between a heaven and hell
which are mirrors of one another. Jabes, is a mirror-
reversal of Lockwood, the elect reprobating the elect. To
phrase this differently, we can say that a Calvinist
language of rejection is doubly built in to the text of
Wuthering Heights: both into the Christian theology which

rebukes the characters' proceedings and into the reflex motion of retaliation which the text sends back to the retributive God. It is the language of eviction, rejection and casting-out which most intensely carries this charge of energy. And most specifically, in a literary dialect whose dynamic—like Milton's—is founded especially in verbs of violent motion, and on nouns whose active character within the sentence impersonates properties common to verbs,[10] *Wuthering Heights'* systole–diastole tension is maintained by *verbs* connoting extrusion.

This principle is a source of the concentrated power of Catherine's narrative of her dream, so focal to the meaning of the novel, in which she is willingly aborted from Heaven by angry angels:

> 'This is nothing,' cried she; 'I was only going to say that heaven did not seem to be my home; and I broke my heart with weeping to come back to earth; and the angels were so angry that they flung me out, into the middle of the heath on the top of Wuthering Heights; where I woke sobbing for joy. That will do to explain my secret, as well as the other. I've no more business to marry Edgar Linton than I have to be in heaven....'
>
> (p. 80)

To present one mystery as an explanation of a deeper one is a favourite practice of the novel. The interpretative dream Catherine supplies is, of course, an heretical revision of Genesis and the fall of man. It reads the fall of woman as a supremely *felix culpa* enabling rite of passage from an alien world of unsympathetic foreigners to the high moor as a place of sanctuary. The dream enacts a myth of return, for in the experience of the human girl with such a temperamental disaffinity with God's Angels earth has predated heaven. In a reversal characteristic of the author, the wilderness (into which our first parents in Genesis and the Israelites in Exodus were ejected) is conceived as a home prior to Eden, back to which all allegiances yearn. Mirror-antagonism is enacted in the very sentence-structure: *I broke my heart with weeping/ I woke sobbing for joy*, where the first paradox—weeping in a happy place—begets a tragicomic second—painful ecstasy. Implicitly, Catherine's fall is from Father-God to Mother Earth: her form of words includes the electric 'H' code which excites in readers a mythic apprehension of the Heights: *heaven— home—heart—heath—Heights*. The alliterative pattern traces the journey down. But when Catherine is 'down', she is paradoxically at the 'Heights', exalted as Lucifer whose rebellion takes him 'into the limits of the north', 'High on a hill, far blazing, as a mount/Raised on a mount' (*PL* V.755, 757–8). The violent exodus of Catherine's rebellious discharge from the community above is mediated by the sudden verb *flung*, with its Miltonic urgency. Verbs denoting violent acts of throwing are familiar in *Wuthering Heights*; in the same chapter, for instance, Heathcliff 'flung himself on a bench' (p. 76) and Catherine 'flung Hareton onto the settle' (p. 83). The dream of the fall remembers Milton: 'Him the almighty power/Hurled headlong' and 'headlong themselves they threw/Down from the verge of heaven' (*PL* I.44–5; VI.864–5)—but compresses the latter's double articulation of the rebels' passive ejection from and active disavowal of Heaven into a single gesture of mutual disinclination. The Christian myth, turned inside-out, is forced into ironic disclosure of its own fatal inconsistencies. What kind of 'Heaven' houses irate angels?

The dispute between Heaven and womankind is focused throughout *Wuthering Heights* in the running quarrel between Joseph and the two Catherines. As 'an elderly, nay, an old man: very old, perhaps, though hale and sinewy' (p. 2), he represents the old, unregenerate

Adam who won't be dispossessed of his garden, the prophet of the Ancient of Days himself; as 'the old hypocrite', 'the elder', 'the wearisomest Pharisee', he stands for the deformity of the Father's world-system and of the social traditions of the fathers, which he vigorously defends. Joseph sublimely demonstrates the implications of the violence and disruption (the language of rejection) which *Wuthering Heights* discerns at the heart of the religion of the Father. As a servant of 'the Lord' whose name he invokes and of the patriarchy, with its laws of inheritance, respect for genealogy and property-based system of kinship in family and tribe, his allegiance is to Hareton as the legitimate 'head of the old family' (p. 196), the namesake of the original builder of the Heights, and the disinherited heir, into whom the old man instils 'a pride of name, and of his lineage' (p. 196). However, the manner in which Joseph elects to inculcate these ancient values into the heir is by encouraging him to go to the bad, in language and behaviour:

> He allowed that he was ruined: that his soul was abandoned to perdition; but then, he reflected that Heathcliff must answer for it. Hareton's blood would be required at his hands; and there lay immense consolation in that thought.
>
> (p. 196)

The servant of God in effect curses the legitimate heir, as his twisted code wrestles the biblical ethic to declare its punitive bias. The formulaic mode of identifying protagonists—a familiar device in the text as a whole— has the effect of universalising activities and relationships. By abstracting Joseph into 'the old man' and Hareton into 'the lad', the narrative distances these representatives of the two generations (in a novel that is supremely concerned with generation-conflict) and formalises them in a set-piece struggle on a cosmic dimension. The 'old man' impersonates on one level the vindictive Ancient of Days: the young man is the falling human son of the Father-God. To vindicate his system the Father-God demolishes it. Both Joseph and Hindley seek to exploit the flaw in the Divine scheme (see p. 133 above). Again, diction is profoundly and revealingly Miltonic:

> Hell heard the unsufferable noise, hell saw
> Heaven ruining from heaven...
> (PL VI.867–8)

The Miltonic Latinism (from *ruinare*, to fall) which converts the normally transitive into an intransitive verb, discloses the violent disruption at the centre of the myth. Heaven is tricked by its own punitive codes into hurting itself. The falling angels are a slab of Heaven parting company with its own coherent structure; their loss impairs the divine perfection. This breach, which Milton's narrative is quick to close up, Emily Brontë's not only leaves wide open but recurrently advertises in parallel circumstances. The 'ruin' of Hindley, Heathcliff and Hareton, while individually and sociologically explicable, is also charged (in so far as the novel rewrites it cyclically as an 'H' coded event) against the Father who is responsible for the state of things in the world below, where the sons are 'abandoned to perdition'.

It is axiomatic in *Wuthering Heights* that those against whom Joseph sets his face in righteous indignation shall count as the reader's friends. Lockwood, believing the honour of his own mother to be impugned by the tirade of 'the aged rascal' (p. 13) against the younger Catherine, has ideas of kicking him out of the door himself. Jehovah's vinegar-faced servant brings in a verdict against not just one but two generations of ungodly womankind: '"Bud yah're a nowt, and it's noa use talking—yah'll niver mend uh yer ill ways, bud goa raight tuh t'divil, like yer mother afore ye!"' (p. 13). From Catherine II back to Catherine I and so on back through the shadowy generations of the mothers to 'our general mother' Eve, *Wuthering Heights* represents the spiritual wisdoms of the male and female as being fundamentally divergent. We note that Catherine skirmishes with Joseph, finally routing him and obtaining his exit, in a language which belongs to him but not to her. The diction of his Church, its primitive sexual fears and defensive codes ironically denounced on her tongue as Babel din, returns his own beliefs against the believer committed to the laws which generate the dynamic of that language. The female tradition is not shown to possess any dogmatic structure of autonomous language in which to declare its wisdoms, as the novel unfolds. The moor is quiet. The intuitions of woman arise from sleep, as vague queries ('"Nelly, do you never dream queer dreams?"' [p. 79]), assertions of inadequacy to speak out fully what is most deeply contained within the breast ('"I cannot express it; but surely you and every body have a notion that there is, or should be...?"' [pp. 81-2]), the resort to natural symbolism ('"moonbeam...lightning"' [p. 80], "the eternal rocks beneath"' [p. 82]), vague intimations of a transcendence beyond words: '"I shall be incomparably beyond and above you all"' (p. 160). A feminine wisdom may be felt to inhere in the scraps of ballad which float out fitfully through Nelly's memory to hint at a music of the spirit prior to and still most deeply underlying the present story: ''Twas far in the night', 'Fairy Annie's Wedding'. But more comprehensively, the whole text of *Wuthering Heights* may be read as an oblique speech of clues, traces and tokens which constitute a kind of cynosure, drawing our eyes toward an area of spiritual knowledge which is generally covered by silence. In so far as it deals with the human experience of loss, it also concerns itself with spiritual loss. Like a dolmen or obelisk it memorialises an ancient religious intuition which lacks a sacred text, Church, creed or archive. Like the fragments of Catherine's diary, the delving beneath the guide-stone which preserves the hoardings of pebbles and snail-shells from Nelly's and Hindley's childhood, the threefold gravestones which mark the vanished characters, the fiction may be read as memorialising a lost source.[11] As the legible if fragmentary record of an illegible underground world of the spirit, *Wuthering Heights* signals to the reader to look subliminally for traces of meaning to supply to the work, in the individual 'world within'.

Seen in this light, the vigorous argument with the God of our Fathers which the novel conducts may be experienced as a gesture of guidance to the 'Heaven on earth' which is ready to receive the Father's rejects. The second Catherine accordingly threatens Joseph with his own whip:

> 'You scandalous old hypocrite!... Are you not afraid of being carried away bodily, whenever you mention the devil's name? I warn you to refrain from provoking me, or I'll ask your abduction as a special favour.'
>
> (p. 13)

She flourishes a 'long, dark book' at him, proposed by her and acknowledged by him as the book of her 'Black Art'. It is her book against his, also aptly 'long and dark', the biblical text which constitutes his armoury of linguistic ammunition. The book of Emily Brontë's own Black Art takes a special relish in the easy routing of woman's preposterous adversary, through the inevitable ricochet-effect of the fear which animates his own vocabulary of aggression:

'Oh, wicked, wicked!' gasped the elder, 'may the Lord deliver us from evil!'

'No, reprobate! you are a castaway—be off, or I'll hurt you seriously! I'll have you all modelled in wax and clay; and the first who passes the limits I fix, shall—I'll not say what he shall be done to—but, you'll see! Go, I'm looking at you!'

(pp. 13–14)

The frightening words for Joseph are those drawn from the lexicon of Calvinism which threatens extrusion. They mark him extraneous to the Father's initial choice or the home-world where he can flourish. He will be *'carried away'*, 'I'll ask your *abduction'*; his caste is that of the *'reprobate... castaway'* (emphasis added). The power of Catherine's eyes is stressed, till Joseph, hurried out by a 'sincere horror' of the evil eye, vacates the room smartly, 'praying and ejaculating "wicked"' as he goes (p. 14).

The mysterious centrality of Joseph in relation to the whole body of the novel may be partly accounted for by the fact that he writes in to the text a whole dialect of malediction which acts as a kind of key metaphoric language in bringing to light the nature of the human condition. His terminology of extrusion and disinheritance touches on the theme always dominant in the first half of *Wuthering Heights*, and still resonant in the second, of the rejected or changeling child. The Calvinist and Lutheran dream—or nightmare—of a Father predestining his children to unmerited reprobation on the one hand and unmerited Grace on the other, which had featured so largely in the Brontë household's scheme of education that even the teapot was religious,[12] provides a speaking analogy to the perplexity all children feel as to whether they are loved and wanted, their fear of the implications of parental anger, the early sense of the loneliness of the self. Anne Brontë's poetry declares the difficult, harrowing search for obedience to a reprobating Godhead, the effort of self-inhibition that goes into abstention from repudiating a divine parenthood so barren of mother-love, so demanding and so liable to turn in incomprehensible antagonism from its children. Her simple, singular quatrains hymn the quality of divine gentleness of which she is so aware as the basis of all human good, but which she fears might be absent in the Father who 'banishes' souls luminous with 'gentle charity' from his heaven. Her beautiful 'Prayer' records:

> Unless Thou hasten to relieve,
> Thy suppliant is a castaway.[13]

Cowper's 'The Castaway' focused for Anne Brontë the possibility of divine inhumanity; the gentle, gracious tones of her poetry stand in judgement of that inhumanity, not with the mutinous defiance of Emily's fetching-up of alternative religion out of the interior of the individual spirit and the dust of the mother-planet, but by carefully redefining and recasting for her Maker's benefit the laws which he himself invented. In this she is as genuinely Miltonic as Emily, but to Emily's Lucifer Anne as 'suppliant' takes up a position as the rightful child of her heavenly Father, that assumed by Milton's Son, in correction of Old Testament logic:

> For should man finally be lost, should man
> Thy creature late so loved, thy youngest son
> Fall circumvented thus by fraud, though joined
> With his own folly? That be from thee far,
> That far be from thee, Father
>
> (PL III.150-4)

To Anne's 'The Father surely cannot hate us', Emily replies 'But he does, and we hate him'. Wuthering Heights is, heard in this mode, the song of Lucifer against Creation.

'I'll ask your abduction!' 'No, reprobate! you are a

castaway—be off...!' Catherine echoes, in a comic
vein, the dilemma of all the novel's characters who find
themselves in a world where the mother-principle is
officially absent from the scheme of creation. The
question, reiterated or implied with varying degrees of
distress throughout the novel is 'Where is our home?'
The profound ambivalence experienced in the novel as
to the whereabouts of home centres in the first
Catherine, in whom Emily Brontë's own heresies (in so
far as we may judge them from the evidence of her lyric
poetry) are most fully articulated, criticised and evalu-
ated. But it is in the figure of Heathcliff that the horror
of expatriation from origins is most bitterly concentrated. When Heathcliff is introduced into the Earnshaw
household, the whole family combines to expel 'it'. The
'dirty, ragged, black-haired child' is fifteen-times-over
'it' in three short paragraphs: 'Mrs. Earnshaw was ready
to fling it out of doors.... Mr. Earnshaw told me to wash
it, and give it clean things, and let it sleep with the
children' (p. 35). Only when the child is christened does
the narrative grudgingly allow 'it' into the collective
human world as 'him' (p. 36). This persistent exclusion
of Heathcliff from human designation—as if the text
sought to close its hospitality against him—symbolically
reflects the hostile reaction of a family group to the birth
of a new sibling.[14] But we note that even when the
foster-child is named, the meaning and status of the
name are dubious and indeterminate, being that of a pre-
deceased legitimate son (hence, an usurped name) and
serving indiscriminately as Christian and surname
(p. 36). The riddling name is therefore a sign of stigma.
We know him, *literally*, by his lack of a name. A precedent
for the experience of disinheritance which grasps the
author's imagination here is to be found in *Paradise Lost*'s
account of the terrible erasure of the fallen angels from
the Book of Life:

of their names in heavenly records now
Be no memorial blotted out and razed
By their rebellion, from the books of life.

(I.361–3)

This elimination of God's discarded sons carries a threat whose potency is perhaps unmatched in all Milton's writings: the Milton who wrote in *Ad Patrem* that his poetry was a way of inscribing *'parentis/Nomen'* (ll. 119–20) on the future for all time, but who significantly failed to address himself *Ad Matrem*. The existence of God's sons is unwritten, or written out and de-secrated; they have no Father, and no past tense. This terrifying liberation from all ties of belonging involves an act of violence toward the communal Memory, committing the disinherited sons to an unintelligible future because it has robbed them of yesterday. Their existence is predicated on non-existence. As absences in God's mind, they cannot know his love, eternally.

This condition of abortion from one's own beginnings, an equation both for mother-loss and for paternal law, is the dominating fear that either vexes or masters the psyche in *Wuthering Heights*. The literary equivalent of such loss is wished on the reader by the novel's retention of vital information. The narrative implicates us in Heathcliff's absence of origins by steadfastly bereaving us of information as to where he came from. Like Byron's Lara, Heathcliff stands to us as well as to his fostering family 'a stranger in this breathing world .... A thing of dark imaginings' (*Lara* I.xviii.315, 317), the concluded tale being 'untold' (II.xxv.627). Without birth-certificate, comprehensible language or personal recommendation, Heathcliff presents a life shorn of testimonials. The novel records a cancelled early childhood, 'blotted out and razed/... from the books of life', an unwritten prehistory which on one level recalls

141

the changeling child of folklore and ballad, bringer of ill-luck from the fairy into the human world; on another it is God's dispossessed son who finds no place to lay his head. *Wuthering Heights*, like *Paradise Lost*, is latent with the compressed energies of the disempowered. It never teaches us to love the reject Heathcliff is, any more than its characters may be said to 'love' him in a conventional sense. Save for his two allegiances, Catherine and Mr Earnshaw, Heathcliff as the equivalent of a damned soul can neither experience nor call forth love, any more than can Milton's fallen angels, severed from their birthright. The signal difference is, of course, that while the spirits of *Paradise Lost* are punished for recognisable acts of mutinous impiety, Heathcliff is being punished for nothing more than the fact of his existence. His progress enacts the Romantic Platonising restatement of Christian myth which sees birth as a fall into matter, pain, loss and mortality.[15] Sentenced to life, Heathcliff's punishment precedes his crimes. His suffering causes rather than succeeds his fall; his mere existence entails a concatenation of other falls.

Heathcliff's life, then, is a paradigm of Calvinist reprobation. Amongst the unwanted masses wandering on the streets of Liverpool, he has the status of human waste material. This thought might well have suggested itself to the inspired Joseph, divinely ventriloquial:

> 'Aw's niver wonder, bud he's at t'bothom uf a bog-hoile. This visitation worn't for nowt, und Aw wod hev ye tuh look aht, Miss,—yah muh be t'next. Thank Hivin for all! All warks togither for gooid tuh them as is chozzen, and piked aht froo' th' rubbidge! Yah knaw whet t'Scripture ses—'
>
> And he began quoting several texts; referring us to the chapters and verses where we might find them. (p. 85)

Mr Earnshaw's apparently random meeting with and preference for the child is a mocking parody of election:

as the reprobated 'rubbidge' whom Joseph expects to end up at the bottom of a providential bog-hole, the text maintains toward him an extraordinary degree of stressful equanimity, robbing the reader of escape into those comforting twin reactions, praise/blame or sympathy/antipathy, by means of which strategies we might form the illusion of a stably definable human relationship with the character, as we feel entitled to do in realistic fiction. Rather, the author keeps him at a riddling and emotionally neutralising distance, as if a scientist's eye were to dissect out and anatomise in print a fragment of the psyche: a unit of living tissue of pain and loss. Heathcliff is Lucifer with the addition of a childhood—a nameless phenomenon for which none of our conditioned emotional responses seems adequate.

Isabella's vindictive account of Heathcliff's hellish condition demonstrates this gap between the character and the reader which the text refuses to mediate. Catherine is dead, and Isabella accuses Heathcliff of having murdered her:

> 'His attention was roused, I saw, for his eyes rained down tears among the ashes, and he drew his breath in suffocating sighs.
>
> 'I stared full at him, and laughed scornfully. The clouded windows of hell flashed a moment towards me; the fiend which usually looked out, however, was so dimmed and drowned that I did not fear to hazard another sound of derision.
>
> 'Get up, and begone out of my sight,' said the mourner.
>
> 'I guessed he uttered those words, at least, though his voice was hardly intelligible.' (p. 180)

In *Paradise Lost*, the devils—parched as Tantalus—are condemned to chew 'bitter ashes' (X.566), their mouths 'With soot and cinders filled' (l. 570). This dry, fruitless straining after a condition of life ineluctably alienated, the sweet, fresh water of life-giving Grace, is enacted too in the imagery of *Wuthering Heights* as a deprivation of elementary succour, in the absence of which the sufferer cannot be said to live at all. The 'rain' of Heathcliff's 'tears among the ashes' transforms simple location—a man weeping over a grate with a spent fire—into an imagist rendering of an inner Gehenna. The chemistry of grief combines the salt of tears with the sterile leavings of the coalfire. This deathly condition is further reinforced by his 'suffocating' breathing, by whose killing inspiration the body fights its own biological inclination to survive. These powerfully emotive elements are, however, curiously nullified at source by a depersonalising blankness of mood in a text which seems to follow a policy of mythologising circumlocution. And that which is written round—never entered into or taken into us—is individual personality. Isabella's account (itself as much a symptom of her own rage as a witness of her subject) is dominated by the cosmic impersonality of its conceits, recording Heathcliff as a kind of weather—rain, cloud, deluge—as an aspect of the Fall (the fiend), and through the formulaic mode of denomination which typifies the manner of *Wuthering Heights*. As 'the mourner', his figure is at once distanced and universalised. The phrase condemns Isabella's mockery, yet it places her victim beyond the reach of her cruelty and and immunises him from our pity. The 'mourner', housed in a self in which he no longer feels at home, attends to the rituals of his own despair in solitary confinement. The multiple lenses through which the narrative-within-a-narrative permits us to spy into privacy and speculate on the identity of the being claimed by choric voices in the novel to be 'not a human being' (p. 172), 'ghoul', 'vampire' (p. 330), also hold us rigidly apart from what we contemplate. The act of reading him hence repeats the reprobation of Heathcliff in our minds.

More speakingly than any other voice in the novel, Heathcliff's blasphemes his Maker, rejecting the conditions of his creation with contempt and repudiating the words of Scripture and the Church, contradicting the Word (p. 334). Conceived as an apostate, he allowed Emily Brontë to unleash her most sacrilegious opinions concerning her father's religion, with the fullest energy and licence, and—premised on this iconoclasm—the shaping-out of an opposite religious intuition:

> 'Whether the angels have fed him, or his kin beneath, I cannot tell; but he has not eaten a meal with us for nearly a week—He has just come home at dawn, and gone upstairs to his chamber; locking himself in—as if any body dreamt of coveting his company! There he has continued praying like a methodist; only the deity he implored was senseless dust and ashes; and God, when addressed, was curiously confounded with his own black father.' (p.173)

Beneath Isabella's spiteful sarcasm, there is a well-relished narrative irony. It assimilates Heathcliff to Joseph, for in praying 'like a Methodist', he impersonates an enthusiasm which (with its Puritan overtones) was an emotive idea for Emily Brontë.[16] Prefiguring the shedding of his tears among the ashes, he invokes a deity of 'senseless dust and ashes', as though the symbolic living fires that warm the world of the Heights had turned to a final cremation. The vitriolic allusion to the Israelites in Exodus and Christ's agony in the wilderness speaks of the provision of manna, the spiritual food of the Chosen. Heathcliff turns from his 'black father' (God or Satan, indiscriminately) to invoke the only God who will choose him: the god of the wilderness, the 'mother in the earth' of Nelly's ballad (see p. 64 above),

Catherine herself, interred within the encroaching moor.

Glories to Sattan

The novel ends in a conclusive articulation of silence as Lockwood 'wondered how any one could ever imagine unquiet slumbers for the sleepers in that quiet earth' (p. 338). Its final clause is structured as a beautiful and harmonious chiasmus: *unquiet: slumbers :: sleepers: quiet.* But the word *unquiet* is implicitly part of a double negative. The narrator finds the state of *un*quiet *un*imaginable. The stress of insoluble ambiguity still resides, of course, in the chiasmus: Lockwood has been known to be wrong, and what he cannot imagine has never been a litmus test for the possible. Yet in this novel, *earth*, which is its final word, has represented the speechlessly underlying finale to human life, the condition of wordlessness which bounds man in infancy and at the end grounds him in terminal silence. *Earth* is the focus of intense desire. 'How beautiful the Earth is still'; 'Cold in the earth'; 'In the earth, the earth, thou shalt be laid'; 'Shall Earth no more inspire thee': embedded in these first lines of some of Emily Brontë's most famous poems the word *earth* discloses itself as one of the artist's most magical initiating terms, from which the poem's creation originates. *Earth* is spell-binding, incantatory to her imagination. It is home, centre, sanctuary. It may feature as the destination at which the poem signals its earliest intention to arrive. Hence, the poem which opens thus:

Often rebuked, yet always back returning
To those first feelings that were born with me

closes thus:

Father-God, Mother Earth

> The earth that wakes *one* human heart to feeling
> Can centre both the worlds of Heaven Hell.

The sacred journey that ends at source, implying the symbol of the circle of Eternity measured upon a radius of Time, is a process within the psyche, which has an innately homing intuition. The antithetically structured first line, incorporating a characteristic inversion of word-order ('back returning'), mimes the habit of retrogression which the poet refuses to deplore. Its pattern of return is the reflex of an outing—a pilgrimage as simple as a country walk—which paradoxically leads in to the earth which is a medial point of stabilisation for the compass-projection of the dynamic polarities of human life (Heaven and Hell). As the last word in *Wuthering Heights*—the novel's destination—earth resolves all grievances without litigation, keeps secrets, rectifies asymmetries and quiets the hectic quarrel of the novel's children. It gathers up and assumes into one another's nature the *dramatis personae*, Edgar Linton, Catherine, Heathcliff, in a threefold union, covering their identity in the heath that overruns the church wall and is in process of obliterating the inscription of their names. To the Father's loud language of rebuke, the mother-world answers not one word, though we may say that she—in the most literal possible sense—undermines his works, reintegrates both his rejects and his chosen few in the same holistic process and activates a principle of continuous recrudescence and recidivism in the works he architects to charter his authority.

In a novel so committed to disorderly conduct, to a Lady of Misrule and a Saturnalian impulse to fell the Mighty and erect the low, the chthonic territory of the natural world may be perceived by the stealthy reader to participate as chief trespasser and saboteur. Nature's procedure in relation to the church is that of an expert in demolition, *Eikonoklastes* subjecting the anachronistic icons to the attrition of seasonal weather till they shatter and vanish, dismissing his dogmas, letting in the fresh air—again, literally— to his unsalubrious ideas. In the course of the novel, the moor is seen to make good progress in restoring the church architecture to its original status. Lockwood notes early in his itinerary,of the Chapel of Gimmerton Sough: 'The roof has been kept whole hitherto, but as the clergyman's stipend is only twenty pounds per annum, and a house with two rooms threatening speedily to determine into one, no clergyman will undertake the duties of pastor' (p. 21). The precarious state of the roof, together with the disposition of the twin-roomed house to echo the major theme by a joyous collapse of two-into-one, is extended at the novel's centre by the careful specifications given for Catherine's burial, in which it appears that the moor is actively engaged in reclaiming the churchyard:

> The place of Catherine's interment, to the surprise of the villagers, was neither in the chapel, under the carved monument of the Lintons, nor yet by the tombs of her own relations, outside. It was dug on a green slope, in a corner of the kirkyard, where the wall is so low that heath and bilberry plants have climbed over it from the moor; and peat mould almost buries it. (p. 168)

Finally, the narrator (having registered the fact that the Kirk is vacant and in disuse [p. 295]), revisiting in 1802 after Heathcliff's death, notes in passing that a moor sheep has got in and is cropping the short turf on the graves (p. 305), then brings his narrative to rest in the churchyard:

> My walk home was lengthened by a diversion in the direction of the kirk. When beneath its walls, I perceived decay had made progress, even in seven months—many a

window showed black gaps deprived of glass; and slates
jutted off, here and there, beyond the right line of the roof,
to be gradually worked off in coming autumn storms.

I sought, and soon discovered, the three head-stones on
the slope next the moor—the middle one grey, and half
buried in heath—Edgar Linton's only harmonised by the
turf, and moss creeping up its foot—Heathcliff's still bare.

(pp. 337-8)

The Sabbath feeling with which the novel concludes is
rooted in imagery of pastoral consummation, the
subversively maternal embrace with which the earth (in
silent disregard of divine opinion and permission) takes
back the dead into a world of absorbent growth. We may
remember the entrance of Milton's Satan into Paradise:

Due entrance he disdained, and in contempt,
At one slight bound high over leaped all bound
Of hill or highest wall

. . .

So clomb this first grand thief into God's fold

(IV.180-2, 192)

The rape of God's pastoral Paradise is reversed in
Wuthering Heights so that the outside world of pastoral
nature (Catherine's 'Heaven') clambers over into the
'hallowed ground' with ease, to do the wordless work of
reclamation. Here the prose licenses the appearance of
purpose and motivation in the insentient and unconscious life of 'heath and bilberry plants' which trespass
over the dividing line which conventionally marks the
limits of the holy. The important work attributed to
nature is erasure in the interests of reintegration. The
signs which formulate Catherine in the conscious world
(the structure of the grave, with its stone and
inscription) are enveloped in a subliminal existence:
'peat mould almost buries it'. The sense of nature's

mysterious benignity in these passages is profound. Dissolution, decomposition, undoing of form are elaborated with a lyricism and vivacity which implies a beneficent process of transformation into a new mode of life more abundant in joyous perception and ease of being. Lockwood's final vision of the church orchestrates this theme as a major and ultimate statement of the novel. If decay can be said to 'make progress' and autumn storms to undertake a fruitful 'work' of gradual demolition, the dismantling of the church comes to seem like an act of clearance, mysteriously correspondent in its air of sacred therapy with the ongoing process of 'harmonisation' in the three graves, which are halfway to becoming indistinguishable.

An effect of this surreptitious narrative subversion of the church so that it reverts to its constituent elements is a displacement of the experience of the holy within the text. The heath becomes, as I have shown (see pp. 87–8 above), despite *animal* nature's implication in a chain of predatory suffering, a sanctuary whose magnetic spiritual attraction for the novel's children is transmitted through them to the reader. The numinous territory which was combined refuge, playground and Sabbath home to the first generation also exerts an electrifying compulsion on the second. The wilderness as focus of desire calls the second Catherine to forsake the fertile and leafy garden-world. Thrushcross irks and provokes a hankering after exodus from the constricting *locus amoenus*, which is made to seem as instinctual as the migratory urge in birds: ' "And what are those golden rocks like, when you stand under them?"... 'And why are they bright so long after it is evening here?"' (p. 189). The childish pertinacity of the inquisition rouses Nelly to pour what she thinks is cold water on Catherine's excitement, but her attempt to ruin the landscape's glamour by scouring the light off the stone only intensifies the child's homing instinct, like a kind of activated nostalgia for things never known in the flesh. And for the reader too those 'bare masses of stone, with hardly enough earth in their clefts to nourish a stunted tree' (p. 189) are inevitably charged with the energy which the first Catherine's language of desire spelt into the massive stability of 'the eternal rocks beneath', functionless and void of beauty except in so far as they furnish the eternal bedrock of life itself: but, in that light, all-important and all-beautiful. To collapse the church into that mythic landscape of circular Time[17] and circulating identity is to return it to a prior world which is both the foundation of the holy and the object of desire. The aura accumulated by the moor in the course of the novel is curiously revealed in the *trompe l'oeuil* effect which convinces many readers that they have observed the major events taking place in the open (as witness films of *Wuthering Heights* which feature panoramic scamperings and sublimities uttered on hilltops): this is hallucination. Most of the first half takes place indoors, the moor being covertly forbidden to the reader's view. It is our vagrant imaginations which respond to the cravings for freedom on the part of the protagonists by lending to the content of the psyche's inner terrain the character of an excursion. The second half of the novel dissipates this charge of passionate desirability, as Homans points out,[18] by frequent description of the natural world.

The novel terminates in pastoral elegy ('the three head-stones on the slope next the moor' [pp. 377-8]) combined with epithalamion (the wedding on New Year's Day). Death and consummation are intrinsically related in a novel which carries the logic of its action across the limitations placed by cultural and religious taboo on where we may extend the continuum of search for those meanings to which life denies conclusive

access. Lockwood early notes the unusual properties of
the soil in the graveyard to which the narrative will
commit its central protagonists: 'We came to the
chapel...it lies in a hollow between two hills—an
elevated hollow—near a swamp whose peaty moisture is
said to answer all the purposes of embalming on the few
corpses desposited there' (p. 21). It is one of this artful
author's suaver touches to introduce this mystery of
preservation as a quaint local item registered in the
meticulous tourist's itinerary, its authority judiciously
modified: '*is said to* answer'. The report is verified when
Heathcliff opens Catherine's grave and her body is
perceived to lie intact after seventeen years in this peat-
world of mummies which entrances the dead in attitudes
of perpetual waiting. Abstracted from Time and
corruption, the beloved features remain, to Heathcliff's
exstasy, 'hers yet' (p. 288). Ariès comments that 'there is
a *miraculum mortuorum* here'.[19] Christian theology is again
reversed: the bodies that await the Last Judgment and
their own physical reconstitution according to Scripture
('And I saw the dead, small and great, stand before God;
and the books were opened...'[Rev. 20 : 12]) are in
Wuthering Heights awaiting mutual dissolution in the
eternal flux of nature, prolonging their earthly affections to eternity. The body of Catherine resembles a
bride awaiting the hour of marriage. The temporary
survival of the cadaver in the soil's procrastinating
chemistry makes this 'quiet earth' a likeness of the
unconscious mind itself, within whose subliminal
repository a rich dream-content is stored for final access.
In a world of infinite losses and unsatisfied needs, earth
in Emily Brontë is the final place of safe-keeping and
security. That we have to go underground to find this
peace and possession does not in any way discompose her.
The mingling of clays in death is celebrated by the novel
as a nuptial consummation, the enviable cessation of

finite being. The verbs which signal this arrest of
conscious life on the surface of the planet—*dissolve,
transform*—seem to relate to a kind of dream-state, in
which decomposition becomes recomposition, an ec-
static diffusion of Being:

> 'And if she had been dissolved into earth, or worse, what
> would you have dreamt of then?' I said.
> 'Of dissolving with her, and being more happy still!' he
> answered. 'Do you suppose I dread any change of that sort?
> I expected such a transformation on raising the lid, but I'm
> better pleased that it should not commence till I share it.'
> (p. 289)

The insistence on indivisible motion into literal participation in the person of the other, imagery not of
connection or penetration but of full becoming, is
curiously reminiscent of the process described by the 17-
year-old Catherine in relation to dreams that have
'"gone through and through me, like wine through
water, and altered the colour of my mind"' (p. 79).
Heathcliff's desire to go through and through Catherine
in the sleep of death, Catherine's intuition that '"I *am*
Heathcliff"', the transfiguring dream that is in solution
with personality till the end of time, are all ways of
figuring a holistic mother-tongue of total acceptance
and familiarity which opposes the analytic Father-
language of judgement, segregation and eviction.

Hence Heathcliff's 'godless indifference' (p. 334) to the
institution of the Church and its rites is understood by
him as a holy and sacramental obligation to Catherine. It
involves one final and essential ritual to make possible
the initiation of the neophyte into his transcendent
union with the beloved: this figures the opening of a
door. Heathcliff vehemently insists to Nelly that the
sexton remove the panel between his and Catherine's
coffins. '"No minister need come; nor need anything be

said over me"' (p. 334). Rite of passage comprehends the removal of a physical barrier but requires no authorising words to indemnify the transition. This refusal on the novel's part of the warrant of legitimating words spoken by an intercessor between the soul and its God may be read as a final ghostly utterance of Emily Brontë's inheritance of extreme heretical Protestantism: that tradition of Protestantism which ultimately was to lead out of the gate of Christianity altogether—the emphasis on personal inspiration, detestation of ecclesiastical forms and liturgies, the licensing of the self and its private language.[20] This was the liberty toward which Milton's life pressed (see pp. 18–22 above); and 'liberty' recurs perpetually as a talismanic conjuring word throughout Emily Brontë's poetry.[21] Heathcliff's recessional in the second half of *Wuthering Heights* takes the form of an arduous extrication of himself from the mesh of a common vision and a received language. The literality of his conception of union in death as the raw intermingling of the decomposing contents of two graves hearkens back to the shared bed of childhood union, with its removable panel. Figuratively, it presents a posthumous marriage, two becoming—in the most inextricable sense possible— one flesh, repudiating the dogmatic interferences of divine sanction but incorporating a silent new testament gospel of mortality: 'For he is our peace, who hath made both one, and hath broken down the middle wall of partition between us' (Ephesians 2 : 14). Hence Heathcliff's insistence on the removal of the panel: his marriage with Catherine can be literally consummated within the secret places of the earth. It is a return to the integrity of source beyond the certificating pronouncements of language.

The powerful association of earth with needed sleep and the dream-world in *Wuthering Heights* is paralleled by a preoccupation with sleep in Emily Brontë poetry which seems to evidence that she was constitutionally a chronic insomniac.[22] Some of her greatest poems are nocturnals, reflecting a night-journey, and exchanging the solar light by which the world reads and transacts its business for a feminine lunar light disclosing an alternative dimension of vision.[23] The highly strung wakefulness of chronic insomnia may well be implied by the poet's reiterated cry for escape from her own 'wild Desires' on the one hand and 'quenchless will' on the other ('The Philosopher's Conclusion': ll.11, 14). The allure of sleep throughout her poetry persists as the only clue to truce between the warring 'Three Gods' (l.17) within the psyche which feature as an introversion of the Christian myth: 'Heaven could not hold them all, and yet/They all are held in me' (ll.19–20). Mingled with the famous Brontë arrogance (the superb challenge to God to hold on to his creation as she can rein in her vital diversity) is the cry of pain as the mortal framework is taxed to the point of breakdown by the force of a creative *psychomachia*. *Wuthering Heights'* impulse toward transcendence parallels this lyric impulse toward sleep and forgetfulness; the turning-away of so many of the poems from their own unrelenting oppositions to the neutrality of abeyance in earth. ' "*O for the time when I shall sleep/Without identity . . .*" '; ' "I'm *tired, tired* of being enclosed here. I'm *wearying* to escape . . .'(p. 160, emphasis added). Both Catherine and Heathcliff in the latter stages of their lives evince intense exhaustion with the vigilance necessary to sustain existence. Heathcliff images his life as like 'bending back a stiff spring' (p. 325). The account of his posthumous search for Catherine is a tale of excruciating insomnia:

'And when I slept in her chamber—I was beaten out of that—I couldn't lie there; for the moment I closed my eyes, she was either outside the window, or sliding back the

155

panels, or entering the room, or even resting her darling head on the same pillow as she did when a child. And I must open my lids to see. And so I opened and closed them a hundred times a-night—to be always disappointed! It racked me! I've often groaned aloud...' (pp. 290-1)

This is close to the experience recorded in 'Often rebuked' of 'visions rising, legion after legion' which 'Bring the unreal world too strangely near' (ll. 7-8). In each case, consciousness has been ransacked by the contents of the unconscious, which spills threateningly across its limits. The busy wraith of Catherine commands a superhuman labour of response; pursuing his schemes of revenge, Heathcliff resembles Hercules for labours but is finally too abstracted by the diversion of his haunting to 'take the trouble to raise my hand' against enemies (p. 323). A source of this obsession with fatigue on his author's part appears to have been her perception of the too thin film guarding the 'real' from the 'unreal' worlds. The invasive imagination rushing in against her equally firm 'stern reason' threatened mental chaos and required a heroically alert posture keeping the nerves at full stretch: like Heathcliff's tough and tense as 'catgut'. *Wuthering Heights* wills its own closure in the grave solution of the distraught, uneven equation of irreconcilables within the mothering earth, where the names are not so much deleted, as in Milton's God's erasure of the fallen angels' memorials 'blotted out and razed/... from the books of life (see p. 141 above) as absorbed and assimilated. The novel evidences, as does the author's short life-history, a profound desire to memorialise, a concern with documentation of the most fragile of life's events (the diary papers of Emily and Anne; Catherine's diary fragments; Emily's addiction to the genre of saga). The concern here is to perpetuate and hoard what is felt to be of value: Heathcliff's 'avarice' is the figure for this desire in the novel. At the same time it observes an impairment and mutilation deep within the fabric of time which focuses the adventure of life as, from its outset, an exhausted quest for its own cessation.

The choric figures in *Wuthering Heights* are telling in this regard: servants, the doctor, the lawyer, the community's executives appointed to keep the body politic healthy and cohesive. Dr Kenneth, announcing the death of Hindley, puts it thus: ' "Well, Nelly.... It's yours and my turn to go into mourning at present. Who's given us the slip now, do you think?" ' (p. 184). The phrase *given us the slip* is pleasantly turned to convey the function of doctor and servant as caretakers of the novel's characters, whose role—as officials to the community, but more deeply as militant gossips arousing, collecting and distributing news, and hence as narrators on behalf of the community—is to conserve the linguistic continuum. Dr Kenneth is appointed to preserve society in a state of health whilst sharing with Nelly the complicit knowledge that the people with whom he has to deal are only citizens of the world on sufferance, their real but covert attachments being to a prior and after-world. Throughout the novel, the moorland features as the fastness for these refugees, a zone which timelessly gathers back the scatterings of human nature from its profitless struggle with temporality.

Readers concur that in the second half of the novel, artistic energy tends to decline. For this very reason it becomes possible to view, through the ebb, something of the ideas submerged and refracted in the imaginative depths of the work. Toward the end, Lockwood has leisure to listen in on a scene at the Heights in which the wisdoms of the mothers and of the fathers contend in explicit debate. Their exchange is mediated through humour, giving vent to an animating burst of Joseph's preposterous energy as he cants and groans out his case against the women in the novel:

> 'It's a blazing shaime, ut Aw cannut oppen t'Blessed Book, bud yah set up them glories tuh Sattan, un' all t'flaysome wickednesses ut iver wer born intuh t'warld! Oh! yah're a raight nowt; un' shoo's another; un' that poor lad 'ull be lost, atween ye. Poor lad!' he added, with a groan; 'he's witched, Aw'm sartin on't! O Lord, judge 'em, fur they's norther law nur justice amang wer rullers!'
>
> 'No! or we should be sitting in flaming fagots, I suppose,' retorted the singer. 'But wisht, old man, and read your Bible like a Christian, and never mind me. This is 'Fairy Annie's Wedding' - a bonny tune - it goes to a dance.' (p. 308)

'Glories to Sattan', the title of the present section, represent Joseph's Puritan objection to the old folk-ballads, to which Nelly is personally partial and on which Emily Brontë's narrative so gratefully draws for its *topoi*, its anonymous manner and its spiritual roots in an animistic and totemic nature. Joseph's objection is made on the traditional Puritan ground of the pagan vanity and immorality of the ballads, linked with a brand of female Satanism which he believes to be rife in the north, and concluding in an equally traditional cry for the censorship of the wicked ballad-mongers, the suppression of local witches and a regicidal dig at the kings of this world: '"O Lord, judge 'em"'. This apocalyptic vehemence is directed primarily against the 'glories to Sattan' as a religious literature (though oral, not written) set up in antagonism to the Bible and an unholy noise which outrages the eardrums of God's elect as he sits down to peruse the Word. In Joseph's attack on the ballad as specifically women's poetry and women's music, the novel gestures at the existence of the two incompatible languages which declare opposing wisdoms and whose implicit dissent forms a major polarity of *Wuthering Heights*. Joseph's sexual terror is, of course, genuinely Miltonic. As a monstrous old Adam, he knows the etymology of Eve and 'evil' so much pageanted by his more learned predecessor (*PL* IX. 1067); as a native Yorkshireman, his folk memory undoubtedly includes the local witchcraft trials of the seventeenth century of which the Lancashire Pendle trial is the best known.[24] His diabolical misogyny, providing light relief throughout the novel (' "if Aw mun hev a *mistress* set o'er my heead, it's loike time tuh be flitting' [p. 141]), includes not only the two Catherines and Isabella but also Nelly. As narrator, her allegiance is always equivocal. She stabilises the novel's wayward raw material and disintegrative emotions, as we have seen (pp. 64–5 above) by appeal to sensibly adult, literate and Christian standards of behaviour. But her voice is equivocal in calling back to spiritual modes of apprehension whose origins predate Christianity and whose faith is separable from the religion of the fathers. As foster-mother to so many of the novel's children, Nelly rocks their cradle and lulls them to sleep, her 'nurslings' (p. 63). In this agency, the narrator substitutes for a universal mother, source of nourishment, care and order. When they die, she closes their eyes. In this function, Nelly is medial between the world of the living and the world beyond. Her mind rests back upon the traditional wisdoms and folk poetry of the mothers of the race: the practical music of lullaby, proverbial and axiomatic codes of behaviour, and that superstitious demonology (associated with witchcraft and faery) which perceived the upper world as a walking-ground for the ghosts of the dead, placable or implacable, and the underworld as linked to man in animistic and reciprocal relation. It is to this matrix of associations that Nelly as singer of ballads and lullabies attaches herself, the 'witching' women who

pass on their culture down the generations upon the
moorland which is the sanctuary of the great Mother, its
chthonic character as sanctuary of the goddess being
doubled by the fact that, in *Wuthering Heights,* the
mothers of the tribe have literally taken up abode in the
underworld. This theme surfaces in the snatch of a
ballad recorded in Scott which the author embeds in the
text while Nelly is singing the baby Hareton to sleep:

> 'It was far in the night, and the bairnies grat,
> The mither beneath the mools heard that' (p. 76)

As *'the singer'* of 'glories to Sattan', with the anonymity of
Emily Brontë's typically formulaic mode of reference to
individuals, Nelly seems at moments to generalise her
nature into the evoking voice of a timeless community.
Here, the ballad symbolism touches the core of meaning
in the novel.[25] The lullaby 'It was far in the night' relates
the story of a mother, dead and buried, who obtains
permission to break across the boundary between the
liminal and subliminal worlds to redress the grievances
of her orphaned children, rejects at the mercy of their
father and cruel stepmother. The ballad may stand as a
parable for Emily Brontë's text: a novel which, in the act
of declaring the extremity of human need and loss,
recording cries loud enough to wake the dead, arouses
an answering myth in a dialect powerful enough to meet
that need, on the page, with joy, in its totality.

Notes

Introduction

1. 'Editor's Preface to the New Edition', printed in *Wuthering Heights*, ed. Ian Jack (Oxford, 1981), p. 366. All citations of the novel refer to this edition.
2. See J. Hillis Miller, '*Wuthering Heights*: Repetition and the Uncanny', in *Fiction and Repetition* (Oxford, 1982), pp. 43–71, for an account of this structure.
3. James H. Kavanagh's Oedipal over-reading of the 'penetralium' of the house (*Emily Brontë* [Oxford, 1985], p. 26) is far less elucidating (because it narrows and closes the interpretation of imagery to a single sexual code of meaning) than Hillis Miller's resolute opening of 'entrance' to an indeterminate complex of meaning.
4. See J. Hillis Miller, p. 51.
5. Elaine Showalter, *A Literature of Their Own: British Novelists from Brontë to Lessing* (Princeton, NJ, 1977), p. 33.
6. See, for instance, Dorothy Van Ghent, *The English Novel: Form and Function* (New York, 1953), pp. 161ff.
7. Unsigned review of *Wuthering Heights*, from *Examiner* (Jan. 1848), printed in Miriam Allott (ed.) *The Brontës: The Critical Heritage* (London and Boston, 1974), p. 222.
8. Unsigned review of *Wuthering Heights*, from *Britannia* (15 Jan. 1848), in Allott, p. 226.

161

9. G.W. Peck, review of *Wuthering Heights*, from *American Review* (June, 1848), vii, in Allott, p. 236.

10. T.W. Reid, 'The Brontë Novels: *Wuthering Heights*', in Allott, p. 400; Peter Bayne, *Two Great Englishwomen: Mrs Browning and Charlotte Brontë* (1881), in Allott, p. 426.

11. See, for instance, Herbert Dingle, 'The Origin of Heathcliff', *Brontë Society Transactions* vol. 16, pp. 131–8; John Daniel, '*Wuthering Heights* and the Idea of Passion', *London Review* (Winter, 1966).

12. C.P. Sanger, *The Structure of 'Wuthering Heights'* (London, 1926); Lord David Cecil, *Early Victorian Novelists* (London, 1934); Van Ghent.

13. Inge-Stina Ewbank, *Their Proper Sphere: A Study of the Brontë Sisters as Early-Victorian Novelists* (London, 1966).

14. Sandra Gilbert and Susan Gubar, *The Madwoman in the Attic: The Woman Writer and the Nineteenth-Century Literary Imagination* (New Haven, Conn., 1979); Harold Bloom, *The Anxiety of Influence* (New York, 1973).

15. Kavanagh, p. 43. The Marxist tradition includes the chapter on *Wuthering Heights* in Arnold Kettle's *An Introduction to the English Novel* (London, 1951) and Terry Eagleton's *Myths of Power: A Marxist Study of the Brontës* (London, 1975).

16. 'Diary Paper, 1841', printed in *The Shakespeare Head Lives and Letters*, Vol. 1, ed. T.J. Wise and J.A. Symington (Oxford, 1932), p. 238. For the story of Emily playing Charles II, see Winifred Gérin, *Emily Brontë: A Biography* (Oxford, 1971), p. 17.

17. Elizabeth Gaskell, *The Life of Charlotte Brontë*, ed. A.J. Shelston (Harmondsworth, 1975), pp. 268–9.

18. See Bayne, in Allott, pp. 426–8.

19. See Dale Spender, *Man Made Language* (London, 1981).

20. *Wuthering Heights*, p. 138 (my italics for emphasis).

21. *Shakespeare Head Lives and Letters*, Vol. 1, p. 124.

22. For authorities on hemispheric specialisation, see J.S. Bruner, *On Knowing: Essays for the Left Hand* (New York, 1965); M. Corballis and I. Beale. *The Psychology of Left and Right* (Hillsdale, NJ, 1976); M. Ferguson, *The Brain Revolution* (New York, 1973); R.L. Gregory, *Eye and Brain: The Psychology of Seeing* (New York, 1973); S.J. Dimond and J.G. Beaumont (ed.) *Hemisphere Function in the Human Brain*, (New York, 1974).

23. Edward Chitham, *A Life of Emily Brontë* (Oxford, 1987), p. 169. He also points out that Emily drew portraits facing to the right, a common characteristic of left-handed artists (Note to Plate 13).
24. See the tables printed by Betty Edwards in *Drawing on the Right Side of the Brain* (London, 1981), pp. 38ff, for this distinction in an accessible form.
25. Gaskell, pp. 230–1.
26. See Charlotte Brontë's letter to W.S. Williams (22 Nov. 1848), *Shakespeare Head Lives and Letters*, Vol. 2, pp. 286–7.
27. Margaret Homans, *Women Writers and Poetic Identity: Dorothy Wordsworth, Emily Brontë and Emily Dickinson* (Princeton, NJ, 1980), p. 131.
28. Carolyn G. Heilbrun, *Towards Androgyny: Aspects of Male and Female in Literature* (London, 1973), p. 81; Barbara Hannah, *Striving Towards Wholeness* (London, 1972), p. 210.
29. Homans, pp. 30–1. References to Milton in the text are all to *Paradise Lost*, ed. Alastair Fowler (London, 1968).
30. *Ibid., passim.*
31. For fuller treatment of Milton's relation with a powerful feminine Muse, see my *The Idea of Woman in Renaissance Literature: The Feminine Reclaimed* (Brighton, 1986), pp. 186–221.
32. R.H. Tawney, *Religion and the Rise of Capitalism* (London, 1926); Christopher Hill, *Society and Puritanism in Pre-Revolutionary England* (London, 1964); *The World Turned Upside Down: Radical Ideas During the English Revolution* (London, 1972); *Milton and the English Revolution* (London and Boston, 1979).
33. William Dell, from *The Building, Beauty, Teaching and Establishment of A Truly Christian and Spiritual Church* (1646); Gerrard Winstanley, *A Watch-Word to the City of London* (1649), in Hill, *The World Turned Upside Down*, pp. 19, 107.
34. John Milton, *Doctrine and Discipline of Divorce* (1644), in the Yale *Complete Prose Works*, Vol. II, p. 228.
35. Hill, *The World Turned Upside Down*, p. 233.
36. Gerrard Winstanley, *The Breaking of the Day of God* (1648), in G.H. Sabine (ed.), *The Works of Gerrard Winstanley, with an Appendix of Documents Relating to the Digger Movement* (New York, 1965), p. 95.
37. *The Mysterie of God*, in Winstanley, pp. 81–2.
38. *Truth Lifting Up Its Head above Scandals* (1649), p. 128.

40. See Hill, *Milton and the English Revolution*, p. 221.
39. The terms in which the youthful George Eliot communicated her duty of church-abstention to her irate father are themselves those of dissenting Christianity: 'if ever I loved you I do so now, if ever I sought to obey the laws of my Creator and to follow duty wherever it may lead me I have that determination now and the consciousness of this will support me though every being on earth were to frown upon me' (see Gordon S. Haight, *George Eliot: A Biography* [Oxford, London and New York, 1968], p. 43, and Ch. 2 *passim*, for his insightful treatment of her religious crisis). The 'laws of my Creator' are the inner law. This law later taught her to accompany her father to church, out of love and respect for him, but to think her own thoughts whilst in the building. It is significant that Emily Brontë made no such concessions.
41. See Gérin, pp. 130, 156.
42. See John 14 : 26 and 5 : 6. I am profoundly grateful to Irene Tayler for sharing with me her insights into the relation between the Muse and the Holy Spirit in the works of the Brontës; and to William B. Hunter for the work we have done together on the Miltonic Muse/Spirit.
43. Patricia Meyer Spacks, *The Female Imagination* (New York, 1975), p. 136.
44. In Stevie Davies, *Emily Brontë: The Artist as a Free Woman* (Manchester, 1983), pp. 95–113, 152–70.
45. Printed in *The Complete Poems of Emily Jane Brontë*, ed. C.W. Hatfield (New York, 1941), p. 166. All references to Emily Brontë's poems are citations of this edition.
46. See Gaskell, p. 379: 'The character of Shirley herself, is Charlotte's representation of Emily...as what Emily Brontë would have been, had she been placed in health and prosperity.'
47. Fuller treatment of this theme will be found in my '*Jane Eyre*: Exile and Grace', *Durham University Journal* (June, 1985), vol. 77, pp. 223–7.
48. Noted by Gilbert and Gubar in *The Madwoman in the Attic*, p. 367. References to *Jane Eyre* are to the edition by Q.D. Leavis (Harmondsworth, 1966).
49. *Shirley*, ed. Herbert Rosengarten and Margaret Smith (Oxford, 1979), p. 361.
50. Hesiod, *Theogony*, ll. 155–6, in *Hesiod and Theognis*, trans and

ed. Dorothea Wender (Harmondsworth, 1973).

51. All references to Byron are to *The Poetical Works of Lord Byron* (London, New York and Toronto, 1945).

52. The Romantic preoccupation with Prometheus as a revolutionary figure, renovating the terms of power, is exemplified in Shelley's *Prometheus Unbound*. Mary Shelley's edition of *Shelley's Poems* had reached the Parsonage by 1839. See Edward Chitham, 'Emily Brontë and Shelley' in *Brontë Facts and Brontë Problems* (London and Basingstoke, 1983), by Chitham and Tom Winnifrith, p. 59. However, his supposition that Emily's 'darling shade' somehow '*is*' Shelley (p. 70) strains credulity.

53. See n. 46 above.

54. See Daphne Athas, 'Goddesses, Heroines and Women Writers', *St Andrew's Review*, vol. 3 (Fall–Winter), pp. 5–13.

55. This equivalence and at-oneness between the mother-goddess and human nature is a familiar mythic archetype in the ancient mother-religions, e.g. the stricken Ceres in the Eleusinian mystery cult (see my *The Idea of Woman in Renaissance Literature*, pp. 17–22, for an account and sources). Here I am not claiming cultic influence on Emily Brontë, but rather the natural coincidence of corresponding clusters of ideas and images around an identical archetype.

Chapter 1

1. See Leo Bersani, *A Future for Astyanax: Character and Desire in Literature* (Boston, 1976), p. 203, for an acute analysis of the familial complex explored by *Wuthering Heights*.

2. See Bersani, pp. 199–203; and Patricia Drechsel Tobin, *Time and the Novel: The Genealogical Imperative* (Princeton, NJ, 1978), pp. 38–9.

3. See Bersani, p. 202.

4. See Alan Kennedy, *Meaning and Signs in Fiction* (London and Basingstoke, 1979), for an account of the relationship between body and spirit in *Wuthering Heights*.

5. See Georges Bataille, *Literature and Evil*, trans. A. Hamilton (New York and London, 1985), p. 24: 'The road to the kingdom of childhood is regained in *the horror of atonement*'. The conflation of the 'tragic domain' and the 'sacred

domain' in terms of which he reads the novel as a modern version of Greek tragedy is profoundly elucidating in terms of the cost paid for the 'innocent' desire to attain the 'forbidden' world of lost childhood.

6. See J. Hillis Miller, pp. 60–2; Bersani, p. 199; Carol Jacobs, 'Wuthering Heights: At the Threshold of Interpretation', Boundary, vol. 27 (Spring, 1979), pp. 49–71, on the function of the names and character displacements.

7. For the childish basis of personality and behaviour in Wuthering Heights, see Jane Miller, Women Writing about Men (London, 1986), p. 82; Irving H. Buchen, 'Emily Brontë and the Metaphysics of Childhood and Love', Nineteenth Century Fiction, vol. 22 (June, 1967), pp. 63–70.

8. Anne Brontë, The Tenant of Wildfell Hall, ed. G.D. Hargreaves (Harmondsworth, 1979), p. 451.

9. See C.F. Keppler, The Literature of the Second Self (Tucson, Arizona, 1972), p. 135, for Heathcliff as a type of the secondary self.

10. See Adrienne Rich, On Lies, Secrets, and Silence: Selected Prose, 1966–1978 (New York, 1979), p. 90: 'The bond between Catherine and Heathcliff is the archetypal bond between the split fragments of the psyche, the masculine and feminine elements ripped apart and longing for reunion'.

11. J. Hillis Miller, p. 62, gives a helpful account of this frantic procedure of duplication.

12. See Gérin, pp. 142, 168–9. Emily's business-ability was, however, more fallible than Gérin implies. Characteristically, her treasure was hoarded once and for all with the original company, regardless of changes in the stock market and in defiance of advice. This conservatism in money matters perfectly parallels her hoarding-instinct as regards emotional loyalties. Heathcliff's 'besetting sin' of avarice displays the author's calm understanding of her own view of loyalty.

13. J. Hillis Miller, p. 67.

14. See D.P. Varma, The Gothic Flame (London, 1957).

15. See Bersani, p. 201.

16. On the Brontës' Calvinist inheritance, see Valentine Cunningham, Everywhere Spoken Against: Dissent in the Victorian Novel (Oxford, 1975). Cunningham makes the important point that it is not the Methodism in the Brontës' background (Tabby was a Methodist, and Patrick

Brontë had strong Wesleyan sympathies and connections) which accounts for the Calvinist influence, but the Cornish Calvinistic Methodism imported by Aunt Branwell in combination with the hellfire theology indigenous in the region.

17. In Davies *Emily Brontë: The Artist as a Free Woman* (Manchester, 1983) pp. 156–7. And see pp. 36–41 below.

Chapter 2

1. See Carl Gustav Jung, *Aion*, in *The Collected Works of C.G. Jung* ed. William McGuire, trans. R.F.C. Hull (London, New York and Princeton, 1939), Vol. 9 (2), for the *anima*; and Emma Jung, *Animus and Anima* (New York, 1957). See also Kathleen Blake, *Love and the Woman Question in Victorian Literature: The Art of Self-Postponement* (Brighton, 1983), who speaks of Catherine's (and Sue Bridehead's) wish to return to childhood as harking back 'to a time before they grew up into sexual and thereby limited beings' (pp. 150–1).

2. References to *Middlemarch* are made to the edition by W.J. Harvey (Harmondsworth, 1965) and to *Daniel Deronda* to that by Barbara Hardy (Harmondsworth, 1967).

3. See Showalter, pp. 21–2, 37–72.

4. See Gillian Beer, *George Eliot* (Brighton, 1986) on *Middlemarch* for an acute and sympathetic study of this process. Beer notes that for George Eliot 'Writing as a woman must mean writing as a human.... Her writing as a woman takes the whole measure of human experience'. Eliot's concern for the (ungendered) soul within society is equalled by Emily Brontë's commitment to the soul within the Creation.

5. 'Often rebuked', line 2; 'Now trust a heart', line 24. I see no reason to doubt the authenticity of this poem as Emily's. See Edward Chitham, 'Often Rebuked ... Emily's After All', *BST*, Part 93, No. 13 of Vol. 18 (1983).

6. One symptom of the complex of determinisms in which Eliot's heroines can only enjoy limited play of will is indicated by the apocalyptic bases of many of the texts.

7. Caroline Cornwallis drew attention to Blackstone's formulation in *The Westminster Review*, Vol. 10 (Oct. 1856), p. 339, 'The Property of Married Women': 'The husband

and wife are one person in law; that is, *the very being or legal existence of the woman is suspended during the marriage'*.

8. 'Aye, there it is!', line 22.
9. E.g. *Middlemarch*, Ch. 83, p. 870, for the apotheosis of Dorothea's 'sobbing, childlike way' of speaking.
10. See also *PL* IX.215–7; Shakespeare, *A Midsummer Night's Dream*, IV.i.48–51.
11. See my *Emily Brontë: The Artist as a Free Woman*, pp. 129–51, for fuller treatment of the theme of the 'feminised' man.
12. The need for authorisation in this late heroine is rooted in the early dependency of the young Marian Evans on the Father's Divine Guidance: 'Alas,I need monitors and I need chastisement', *The George Eliot Letters*, ed. Gordon S. Haight (New Haven and London, 1954–6), Vol. 1, p. 100.
13. The word 'mellow' seems to have expressed in a peculiarly emotive way the halcyon climate of receptiveness in the psyche which preluded poetic inspiration. In September 1840, she revised a fragment written in May ('Tis moonlight, summer moonlight') which became 'The Night-Wind' ('In summer's mellow midnight'), a striking account of the creative process which fuses peaceful and life-threatening connotations, as in Heathcliff's visitation.
14. Sydney Dobell, Unsigned review, *Palladium* (September 1850), in Allott, p. 278.
15. See C.I. Patterson, 'Empathy and the Daemonic in *Wuthering Heights'*, in *The English Novel in the Nineteenth Century: Essays* (Urbana, 1972), for application of this useful distinction between the pre-moral and the immoral.
16. Virginia Woolf, *'Jane Eyre* and *Wuthering Heights'*, in *Collected Essays*, Vol. 1, ed. Leonard Woolf (London, 1966), p. 189.
17. See Ch. 2, n. 4, above.
18. Plato, *The Symposium*.
19. See Gérin, p. 81.
20. *Ibid.*, p. 110.
21. See Eva Figes, *Sex and Subterfuge: Women Novelists to 1850* (London, 1982), p. 10, for Emily Brontë's 'Darwinism'.
22. See my *Emily Brontë: The Artist as a Free Woman*, pp. 96–7.
23. This principle of fluent amity between the upper and lower worlds is another feature of Emily Brontë's personal religious vision which archetypally resembles the mother religions of antiquity. See *To Eleusinian Demeter*

in *The Orphic Hymns*, trans. A.N. Athanassakis (Missoula Montana, 1977), Claudian, *De Raptu Proserpinae*, in *Claudian*, trans. Maurice Platnauer (Cambridge, Mass., and London, 1922), Vol. 2, for this compact between human nature as an aspect of the natural world and the *una dea* of the lower world. I am not, however, suggesting arcane or cultic influence, as Avrom Fleischman does with Gnosticism, Catharism and alchemy in *Fiction and the Ways of Knowing: Essays on British Novelists* (Austin and London, 1978), pp. 43–8. See Introduction, n. 55, above.

24. E.M. Forster, *A Passage to India* (Harmondsworth, 1961), p. 38.
25. The best applied account of this theory known to me is in Cynthia Griffin Woolf's *Emily Dickinson* (New York, 1986), pp. 54–67, 136–7.
26. *Ibid.*, p. 503.

Chapter 3

1. See Gérin, pp. 44, 45.
2. See Bersani, p. 205.
3. See also Milton's account of Genesis 6:2–4, in *PL* XI.556–633, which attributes the ruin of the 'Sons of God' (allegorically interpreted as the tribe of Seth) to these 'fair atheists' (l. 625).
4. Cecil, pp. 160ff.
5. For the Byronic and Shelleyan variants on the Romantic *Doppelgänger* as 'epipsyche', see Charles E. Robinson, *Shelley and Byron: The Snake and Eagle Wreathed in Flight* (Baltimore and London, 1976), pp. 44–5.
6. *Epipsychidion*, line 52, in *The Complete Poetical Works of Percy Bysshe Shelley* (London, New York and Toronto, 1934), ed. Thomas Hutchinson.
7. The major text, of course, is Matthew 18. See Edgar F. Shannon, 'Lockwood's Dreams and the Exegesis of *Wuthering Heights*', *Nineteenth Century Fiction*, 14 (Sept. 1959), pp. 95–109.
8. Extract from Prefatory Note to 'Selections from Poems by Ellis Bell', in *Wuthering Heights*, ed. Jack, p. 370.
9. 'A.A.A.' ('Sleep not, dream not'), lines 17–18.
10. 'Shed no tears o'er that tomb', lines 31–2.

11. I have treated the Miltonic Eve and the terms of political power more fully in *Images of Kingship in 'Paradise Lost': Milton's Politics and Christian Liberty* (Missouri, 1983), pp. 196–204.
12. 'Editor's Preface to the New Edition of *Wuthering Heights*', in *Wuthering Heights*, ed. Jack, p. 367.
13. Frank Kermode, *The Genesis of Secrecy: On the Interpretation of Narrative* (Cambridge, Mass., and London, 1979), p. 18.
14. See Keith Sagar's reflections on this tradition in 'The Originality of *Wuthering Heights*' in Anne Smith (ed.) *The Art of Emily Bronte* (London and Totowa, 1976), pp. 131ff.
15. See Homans, pp. 104–61 for full, if biased, treatment of this Muse-figure in the poetry.

Chapter 4

1. Martin Luther, *De Servo Arbitrio* (1525), in *Luther and Erasmus: Free Will and Salvation*, trans. and ed. E. Gordon Rupp *et al.* (London, 1969), pp. 138, 206–7.
2. *Ibid.*, p. 230.
3. *Ibid.*, p. 244.
4. Elizabeth Gaskell's account of local religious history in *The Life of Charlotte Brontë* has never been bettered (see pp. 60–76). See also *The Life of Jabez Bunting, D.D., With Notices of Contemporary Persons and Events*, ed. T.P. Bunting, 2 vols (London, 1859).
5. See Valentine Cunningham, *Everywhere Spoken Against: Dissent in the Victorian Novel* (Oxford, 1975), p. 115.
6. *Ibid.*, see p. 114.
7. Luther, p. 230.
8. Job 7 : 10; 2 Samuel 12 : 7; Psalm 149 : 9; Genesis 16 : 12; Isaiah 19 : 2; Zechariah 8 : 10.
9. See Frank Kermode, *The Genesis of Secrecy*, pp. 23–4, for the parabolic nature of interpretation, and the closeness between dream interpretation and the interpretation of parable.
10. For these Miltonic qualities, see Christopher Ricks, *Milton's Grand Style* (Oxford, 1983).
11. See J. Hillis Miller, pp. 64–9.
12. See Phyllis Bentley, *The Brontës and Their World* (London, 1969), p. 42, for a picture of this famous teapot, whose motto reads, 'To me To live is Christ, To die is Gain'.

13. 'A Prayer', lines 7–8, in *The Poems of Anne Brontë*, ed. Edward Chitham (London, 1979), pp. 71, 169.
14. Bersani, p. 205.
15. We may compare Heathcliff's fall into life with the plight of the incarnated soul in Wordsworth's *Immortality Ode* or Shelley's *Adonais*.
16. See e.g. her poem 'A.A.A.', lines 9–14, for the *topos* of the child as doomed 'enthusiast'.
17. The mythic quality of the time experienced in the first half of the novel is obliquely expressed in Lockwood's 'time stagnates here' (p. 27). See also P.D. Tobin, *Time and the Novel* (Princeton, NJ, 1978), p. 39.
18. Margaret Homans, 'Repression and Sublimation of Nature in *Wuthering Heights*', *PMLA*, vol. 93 (January, 1978), pp. 9–19.
19. See Philippe Ariès, *The Hour of Our Death* (1977), trans. Helen Weaver (Harmondsworth, 1983), p. 445. The distinction of the soil, the final ecstasy of Heathcliff resembling that of a demonic saint, and the intactness of the body all point to an heretical secularisation of Christian miracle.
20. See pp. 19–22 above. For the individual sanction of Truth, see Milton's exposition of the terms of belief in *Areopagitica*: 'A man may be a heretick in the truth, and if he beleeve things only because his Pastor sayes so, or the Assembly so determins, without knowing other reason, though his belief be true, yet the very truth he holds, becomes his heresie' *Complete Prose Works*, Vol. 2, ed. Ernest Sirluck (New Haven, 1959), p. 543.
21. It features heavily as the emphatic rhyme word, e.g. 'Riches I hold in light esteem' (l. 8); 'Julian M. and A.G. Rochelle' (l. 68).
22. See Edward Chitham, 'The Development of "Vision" in Emily Brontë's Poems', in Chitham's and Tom Winnifrith's *Brontë Facts and Brontë Problems*, pp. 110–27, for an analysis of Emily Brontë's night-experience (nightmares and probably insomnia).
23. E.g. 'Aye, There It Is!', 'How Clear She Shines', and especially 'Ah! Why Because the Dazzling Sun', for a straightforward reversal of the human preference for day over night.
24. See Kathleen Eyre, *Witchcraft in Lancashire* (Clapham, 1979).

Select Bibliography

Allott, Miriam (ed.) *The Brontës: The Critical Heritage*, London and Boston, 1974.

Aries, Philippe, *The Hour of Our Death*, trans. Helen Weaver, Harmondsworth, 1983.

Bataille, Georges, *Literature and Evil*, trans. A. Hamilton, New York and London, 1985.

Beale, I., *The Psychology of Left and Right*, Hillsdale, NJ, 1976.

Beer, Gillian, *George Eliot*, Brighton, 1986.

Bersani, Leo, *A Future for Astyanax: Character and Desire in Literature*, Boston, 1976.

Blake, Kathleen, *Love and the Woman Question in Victorian Literature: The Art of Self-Postponement*, Brighton, 1983.

Brontë, Anne, *The Tenant of Wildfell Hall*, ed. G.D. Hargreaves, with intro. by Winifred Gérin, Harmondsworth, 1979.

———— *The Poems of Anne Brontë*, ed. Edward Chitham, London, 1979.

Brontë, Charlotte, *Jane Eyre*, ed. Q.D. Leavis, Harmondsworth, 1966.

———— *Shirley*, ed. Herbert Rosengarten and Margaret

Smith, Oxford, 1979.

Brontë, Emily, *Wuthering Heights*, ed. Ian Jack, Oxford, 1981.

—— *The Complete Poems of Emily Jane Brontë*, ed. C.W. Hatfield, New York, 1941.

Byron, George Gordon, Lord, *The Poetical Works of Lord Byron*, London, New York and Toronto, 1945.

Cecil, Lord David, *Early Victorian Novelists*, London, 1934.

Chitham, Edward, *A Life of Emily Brontë*, Oxford, 1987.

Chitham, Edward, and Winnifrith, Tom, *Brontë Facts and Brontë Problems*, London and Basingstoke, 1983.

Cunningham, Valentine, *Everywhere Spoken Against: Dissent in the Victorian Novel*, Oxford, 1975.

Davies, Stevie, *Emily Brontë. The Artist as a Free Woman*, Manchester, 1983.

—— *The Idea of Woman in Renaissance Literature: The Feminine Reclaimed*, Brighton and Kentucky, 1986.

Eliot, George, *Middlemarch*, ed. W.J. Harvey, Harmondsworth, 1965.

—— *Daniel Deronda*, ed. Barbara Hardy, Harmondsworth, 1967.

Ewbank, Inge-Stina, *Their Proper Sphere: A Study of the Brontës as Early-Victorian Novelists*, London, 1966.

Figes, Eva, *Sex and Subterfuge: Women Novelists to 1850*, London, 1982.

Fleishman, Avrom, *Fiction and the Ways of Knowing*, Austin, Texas, 1978.

Forster, E.M., *A Passage to India*, Harmondsworth, 1961.

Gaskell, Elizabeth, *The Life of Charlotte Brontë*, ed. A.J. Shelston, Harmondsworth, 1975.

Gérin, Winifred, *Emily Brontë: A Biography*, Oxford, 1978.

Gilbert, Sandra, and Gubar, Susan, *The Madwoman in the Attic: The Woman Writer and the Nineteenth-Century Imagination*, New Haven, Conn., 1979.

Haight, Gordon S., *George Eliot: A Biography*, Oxford, London and New York, 1968.

Hannah, Barbara, *Striving Toward Wholeness*, London, 1972.

Heilbrun, Carolyn G., *Towards Androgyny: Aspects of Male*

and Female in Literature, London, 1973.

Hill, Christopher, *The World Turned Upside Down: Radical Ideas During the English Revolution*, London, 1972.

Homans, Margaret, *Women Writers and Poetic Identity: Dorothy Wordsworth, Emily Brontë and Emily Dickinson*, Princeton, 1980.

Jung, Emma, *Animus and Anima*, New York, 1957.

Kavanagh, James H., *Emily Brontë*, Oxford, 1985.

Kennedy, Alan, *Meaning and Signs in Fiction*, London and Basingstoke, 1979.

Keppler, C.F., *The Literature of the Second Self*, Tucson, Arizona, 1972.

Kermode, Frank, *The Genesis of Secrecy: On the Interpretation of Narrative*. Cambridge, Mass., and London, 1979.

Luther, Martin, *De Servo Arbitrio*, in Luther and Erasmus, *Free Will and Salvation*, trans. and ed. E. Gordon Rupp *et al.*, London, 1969.

Miller, Jane, *Women Writing about Men*, London, 1986.

Miller, J. Hillis, *Fiction and Repetition*, Oxford, 1982.

Milton, John, *Paradise Lost*, ed. Alastair Fowler, London, 1968.

―――― *Complete Prose Works*, 8 vols, ed. Don M. Wolfe, Columbia, 1953–82.

Rich, Adrienne, *On Lies, Secrets, and Silence: Selected Prose, 1966–1978*, New York, 1979.

Sanger, C.P., *The Structure of 'Wuthering Heights'*, London, 1926.

Shelley, Percy Byssche, *The Complete Poetical Works*, ed. Thomas Hutchinson, London, New York and Toronto, 1934.

Showalter, Elaine, *A Literature of Their Own: British Novelists from Brontë to Lessing*, Princeton, NJ, 1977.

Smith, Anne (ed.), *The Art of Emily Brontë*, London and Totowa, 1976.

Spacks, Patricia Meyer, *The Female Imagination*, New York, 1975.

Spender, Dale, *Man Made Language*, London, 1981.

Tobin, Patricia Drechsel, *Time and the Novel: The Genealogical Imperative*, Princeton, NJ, 1978.

Van Ghent, Dorothy, *The English Novel: Form and Function*, New York, 1953.

Winstanley, Gerrard, *The Works of Gerrard Winstanley, with an Appendix of Documents Relating to the Digger Movement*, ed. G.H. Sabine, New York, 1965.

Woolf, Cynthia Griffin, *Emily Dickinson*, New York, 1986.

Woolf, Virginia, *Collected Essays*, 2 vols, ed. Leonard Woolf, London, 1966.

Index

Index